CREATING CREDIBILITY

LEGITIMACY AND ACCOUNTABILITY FOR TRANSNATIONAL CIVIL SOCIETY

by

L. David Brown

Kumarian Press
An Imprint of Stylus Publishing

Creating Credibility
Published in 2008 in the United States of America by Kumarian Press
22883 Quicksilver Drive, Sterling, VA 20166-2012 USA

The text of this book is set in 10/12.5 New Baskerville

Proofread by Publication Services, Inc.
Index by Publication Services, Inc.

Production and design by Publication Services, Inc.

Printed in the United States of America by Thomson-Shore, Inc.
Text printed with vegetable oil-based ink.

∞ The paper used in this publication meets the minimum requirements of
the American National Standard for Information Sciences-Permanence of
Paper for printed Library Materials, ANSI Z39.48-1984

Library of Congress Cataloging-in-Publication Data
Brown, L. David (Lloyd David), 1941-
   Creating credibility : legitimacy and accountability for transnational
civil society / by L. David Brown.
    p. cm.
   Includes bibliographical references.
   ISBN 978-1-56549-263-9 (pbk. : alk. paper) — ISBN 978-1-56549-264-6
(cloth : alk. paper)
   1. Civil society. 2. International organization. 3. Non-governmental
organizations. 4. Responsibility—Political aspects. 5. Responsibility—Social
aspects. I. Title.
   JC337.B76 2008
   300—dc22
                                       2008010157

To Civil Society Activists
Working for a Better World
Everywhere

Contents

Acknowledgments

I first began to grapple with the issues of civil society legitimacy and accountability more than a decade ago when Jonny Fox and I coordinated a series of studies of NGO and social movement campaigns to influence World Bank projects and policies. In exploring those "struggles for accountability" I began to understand how credibility challenges can become central for civil society organizations.

Soon after I came to the Hauser Center, I coordinated a series of explorations of credibility issues with international NGOs. An initial project examined accountability issues faced by international NGOs based in Japan and the United States. Our Japanese partners, Professors Tatsuya Watanabe and Takayoshi Amenomori, and leaders from several Japanese NGOs educated me about Japanese perspectives on the issue, and leaders from U.S. NGOs provided their perspectives as well. A second project, in partnership with the CIVICUS World Alliance for Citizen Participation, examined experience with credibility issues around the world and began to disseminate ideas and innovations for dealing with them. I am indebted to Finn Heinrich, David Kalete, and Kumi Naidoo at CIVICUS and to Jagadananda at the Center for Youth and Social Development for their contributions to my understanding of credibility innovations around the world. The Sasakawa Peace Foundation supported both these projects, and I am very grateful to the Foundation and its program officers, Yayoi Tanaka and Taka Nanri, for supporting much of the work on which this book is based.

In another initiative, CIVICUS and the Hauser Center convened and facilitated annual workshops for leaders of international advocacy organizations and networks (IANGOs). The IANGO Workshop meetings offered opportunities for chief executives to learn from each other's experience and to grapple with shared challenges. The Workshop identified credibility as a critical issue at its first meeting, and over the next three years its members developed an International NGO Accountability Charter (discussed in Chapter Six). I am indebted to Workshop members and particularly to Peter Eigen, Burkhard Gnaerig, Jeremy Hobbs, Irene Khan, and Gerd Leipold for their insights.

I have been granted opportunities to present and discuss many elements of this book at too many conferences and university seminars to list. Participation in those events has been very helpful in crystallizing many of the ideas presented here.

The Hauser Center has been a wonderful place to pursue these projects. It has provided a lively and creative community of colleagues with very diverse perspectives in which to debate emerging ideas. Mark Moore and Jim Honan were vital to the various legitimacy and accountability projects, and Srilatha Batliwala and Sanjeev Khagram were central to convening and facilitating the IANGOs Workshop. Sarah Alvord, Marais Canali, and Erin Belitskus played pivotal roles in organizing and supporting the early projects. Laura Ax has been invaluable as a project manager and as an editor of this book.

Many colleagues offered stimulating reactions to initial drafts. Srilatha Batliwala, Jane Covey, Alnoor Ebrahim, Jim Honan, Joel Lamstein, Gerd Leipold, and Mark Moore have provided feedback from academic and practitioner perspectives. I have not always taken their advice, but I have always appreciated it. The final version has been much improved by their ideas, though of course I retain responsibility for the remaining errors in thought or fact.

I have also been the beneficiary of monthly discussions with the Brookline Circle, a "spiritual study group" of colleagues interested in organizational and social development as well as the personal journeys of its members. Lee Bolman, Tim Hall, Todd Jick, Adam Kahane, Bill Kahn, Phil Mirvis, and Barry Oshry have continued to support, challenge, humor, tease and advise me (and each other) for almost thirty years.

Last but hardly least, my spouse, Jane Covey, has made writing this book, and much else in my life, possible. She has tolerated absence, inattention, grumpiness, and endless hours of monopolizing computers. She has tactfully suggested that my more convoluted flights of academic jargon might be lost on audiences I want to reach. And she has had faith that I had something to say even when I was not so sure. This book (not to mention the rest of my life) would be very different without her humor, challenge, and support.

List of Illustrations

CHAPTER ONE

Civil Society Legitimacy and Accountability

Civil society includes a wide range of organizations and associations that are organized around values and visions that mobilize social energies. These organizations include nonprofit and nongovernmental organizations (NGOs), churches, unions, professional networks, social movements, art museums, and neighborhood associations. Civil society organizations (CSOs) can be distinguished from the government agencies of the state sector, the corporations and businesses of the market sector, and the kinship networks of the family sector.[1] In the last two decades, CSOs have emerged as central actors in governance and social problem solving on many different issues in many countries and regions. Some of the most widely visible CSOs work across national and regional boundaries to respond to problems that have not been solved by existing transnational institutions.

The International Campaign to Ban Landmines, for example, was launched in 1992 by six CSOs concerned with the devastating impact of landmines, which often persists long after the conflict that spawned them is over. The Campaign sought an international ban on the production and use of landmines. They also sought an international fund to support victims and promote landmine clearance, with mandatory contributions to come from countries that produced and disseminated mines. They recruited other NGOs to organize national campaigns, raise public awareness of the consequences of current landmine policies, and build support in many countries for a total ban. Within a few years, more than 300 civil society organizations and a number of governments had agreed to support a total ban on landmines. In 1997, in spite of determined resistance from several large countries including the United States, 122 countries signed a treaty in Ottawa banning landmines. Later that year the Campaign and its coordinator, Jody Williams, were awarded the Nobel Peace Prize. At that time, the Campaign could not accept the check, since it had neither a formal legal existence nor a bank account.[2]

In order to have impacts like this, CSOs must establish their credibility as international actors whose views are important for other international actors and decisions. *Credibility* refers to attributes such as trustworthiness and believability in the eyes of other actors.[3] This analysis focuses on two aspects of credibility for CSOs: their legitimacy in the wider context and their accountability to key stakeholders. *Legitimacy* means that CSOs are seen to be appropriate and accepted actors, whose activities can be justified in terms of the values, norms, laws, and expectations of their social contexts. The Landmines Campaign solved the legitimacy problem—the Nobel Prize is an impressive recognition of the global credibility and acceptance it had gained by the end of 1997. But the Campaign did not start out as a Nobel Prize winner. It had to mobilize widespread public recognition of and concern for the disastrous consequences of landmines in many countries, and then use that awareness to encourage skeptical governments to participate in a transnational treaty-making process.

Accountability refers to the obligation to answer for one's performance to stakeholders who can reward or punish it. Clear accountability to some stakeholders can create or reinforce an organization's legitimacy. The Landmines Campaign sought to establish new standards of accountability for the producers and users of landmines. But to accomplish that goal, the Campaign itself had to be accountable to important performance standards, such as providing high-quality research information, competent policy analysis, and persuasive recommendations. Accountability is often complex for CSOs. Unlike businesses' accountability to owners or governments' primary accountability to voters, CSOs' accountability is often fragmented among many stakeholders—beneficiaries, donors, regulators, staffs, and allies.

In many countries, CSOs are more trusted by the general public than are many other agencies, including business and government.[4] This trust appears to be grounded, at least in part, in the fact that civil society leaders have less to gain in abusing their positions: Business leaders might maximize their own gains at the expense of the business or its customers, and government officials might use their power in their own self-interest without careful controls. CSOs, on the other hand, depend on their reputations for probity and performance to mobilize resources. They have fewer opportunities to convert resources into self-oriented uses. On the other hand, recent experience suggests that some civil society leaders may also be guilty of self-interested behavior, even though the rewards may be less dramatic than they are in other sectors.

As civil society actors have become more visible and more influential in national and international affairs, more questions have been raised about their legitimacy and accountability. *This book proposes concepts for understanding civil society legitimacy and accountability, particularly in transnational contexts, and it develops approaches to assessing and enhancing the legitimacy and accountability of civil society organizations and interorganizational domains.* This framework is intended to be useful to leaders concerned with challenges to civil society credibility and to researchers interested in the roles of civil society in the transnational context.

This chapter briefly explores why the credibility of CSOs has come under challenge in the last few years, the sources of standards for legitimacy and accountability, and the centrality of civil society values, missions, and strategies for establishing the organizations' credibility. It describes the special challenges faced by CSOs concerned with transnational activity, reviews the central argument of the book, and explains how the book is organized to advance that argument.

Why Legitimacy and Accountability Now?

Why are credibility issues problematic for CSOs? In part the issues are inherent in the nature of civil society. In part they are a result of circumstances that have emerged in the last twenty-five years.[5]

The *nature of civil society* contributes to questions about legitimacy and accountability in several ways. First, CSOs often mobilize people and resources through commitments to social values and missions that are considered to enhance the public good. Their reputations as legitimate and accountable stewards of those missions are vital to their ability to recruit staff and allies to their causes. Mahatma Gandhi and the Indian Independence Movement, Martin Luther King, Jr., and the Civil Rights Movement, and Lech Wałęsa and the Solidarity Movement all depended on their legitimacy as embodiments of widely held social values to mobilize support and credibility. If CSOs leave questions about their legitimacy and accountability unanswered, they risk undermining organizational identities and resources that depend on values and voluntary commitments.

A second common attribute of CSOs is that they have diverse stakeholders that make competing accountability claims. Unlike a corporation, which is ultimately accountable to owners and shareholders, or a democratic government, which is accountable to voters, CSOs are not primarily accountable to any clearly defined stakeholders. They are accountable to donors for their resources, to clients for delivery of goods and services, to allies for performance of joint activities, to staff and members for meeting expectations, and to government agencies for complying with regulations. They are also accountable to their own core values and missions. Dealing with diverse accountability claims may be difficult or impossible when those stakeholders have different or contradictory interests. So accountability is a challenging problem for CSOs because of their relations to many stakeholders.[6]

A third attribute of many CSOs is their predilection for taking up issues on behalf of groups that are poor or otherwise marginalized. While this commitment can be the basis for raising funds and support from charitable donations, it may also require challenging powerful constituencies whose interests are well served by the status quo. Those constituencies may see such challenges as irresponsible or unwise at best: Gandhi, King, and Wałęsa all took on powerful actors who regarded their criticisms as illegitimate if not outright subversive.

Issues of civil society legitimacy and accountability are also a result of *current forces and issues* that have emerged over the last decade. First, many questions about civil society reflect concerns about the legitimacy and accountability of a wide range of institutions. Public distrust that arises from corruption in government agencies or unacceptable practices by business organizations is often as urgent as concerns about civil society.[7] Illegal activities at Enron in the United States or Bofors in India raise questions about both business and government accountability and affect public perceptions of many institutions. In part the growing concern about legitimacy and accountability in CSOs reflects the general "crisis of governance" for many institutions.

Second, some credibility questions grow out of problematic behavior on the part of some CSOs. Publicity about alleged board self-dealing at the Nature Conservancy or Greenpeace's errors in analyzing the Brent Spar oil rig in the North Sea raise questions about whether CSOs live up to their professed values and whether mechanisms exist to enforce minimum standards of practice. CSOs, like many other organizations, are not uniformly altruistic, nor are their actions always consistent with their values.[8] Some challenges to CSO legitimacy grow out of their own behavior.

Third, some current challenges to CSO legitimacy and accountability come from the growing number of agencies that have been targets of civil society campaigns. When CSOs exert political and social pressure on powerful interests, they sometimes provoke counterattacks. Government agencies charged with corruption, corporations criticized for business practices, and intergovernmental institutions challenged to alter projects or policies have often questioned the legitimacy and the accountability of their CSO challengers.[9] It is important that CSOs explain their legitimacy and accountability to key stakeholders, but sometimes those criticisms are inspired by self-interested motives.

All these demands on CSOs have been further complicated by their expanding roles in social development and change. Civil society actors in the past have often been seen as "gap fillers," providing services not available from the market or the state. However, in recent years they have increasingly taken on capacity building and policy advocacy roles that make them participants in multisectoral governance processes.[10] While much civil society work has historically been focused on local problems, CSOs now increasingly work at national and transnational levels as well.[11]

Figure 1.1 Sources of Legitimacy and Accountability Questions

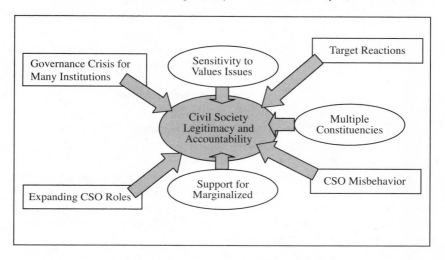

Their emerging roles in large-scale initiatives require new attention to the issues of legitimacy and accountability.

These factors are summarized in Figure 1.1. Factors inherent in the nature of civil society are in ovals close to the legitimacy and accountability issue; factors that have emerged in recent years are in rectangles slightly further from the center. In many cases they are related, of course. In general, the more factors that are pertinent to a given CSO, the more the need for attention to legitimacy and accountability issues. These forces may be particularly important in areas of complex and polarized social problems with relatively few effective institutionalized arrangements for problem solving. Thus emerging problems in transnational contexts, for example, offer fertile areas for civil society intervention, but they are also areas in which legitimacy and accountability questions are particularly acute.

Sources of Legitimacy and Accountability

Expectations about legitimacy and accountability can emerge at several levels of analysis. Perhaps the best understood level is the articulation of *societal ideals* that are established by laws or widely held social norms and expectations. CSOs are expected to obey basic laws and norms of the societies in which they are embedded, and governments or public opinion may set more specific expectations to regulate their formation, resources, and activities. When a government legislates standards, those standards become legal expectations for civil society. Strongly held social norms and "customs having the force of law" may also become societal ideals. When very high salaries for chief executives of some charitable organizations in the United States became public knowledge, for example, the legitimacy of those organizations declined because those salaries violated widely held expectations about "reasonable compensation" in tax-exempt charitable agencies.

Rigorous state regulation of CSOs has been relatively infrequent, however. In part this lack of attention reflects civil society's relative obscurity in many countries. It may also reflect interest in preserving the flexibility and ease of entry that enable civil societies to be a source of social energy and innovation. But in many countries, concern with regulating CSOs has increased as their activities have become more influential and they have become more visible. Initiatives to create restrictive legislation by many governments have created concern among CSOs. Accountability has emerged in the last five years as one of the most important challenges facing civil societies around the world.[12]

Where societal ideals remain ill-defined, groups of organizations concerned with some common area of activity may agree on *negotiated domain standards* that mobilize their combined experience to define legitimate practices and set standards of accountability. The resulting standards may be used to govern the behavior of domain members, even without the standards being embedded in formal legislation backed by the power of the state. Agreement within the domain may be a basis for building wider agreement with other stakeholders in the longer term.

Standards can be negotiated to set accountability expectations in different forms of multiorganization domains. Communities of organizations that carry out similar activities can set standards to define legitimate behavior in that *sector domain*. The Credibility Alliance in India, for example, has convened a nationwide series of consultations to develop standards for Indian development NGOs.[13] Coalitions of actors at different levels, from the local to the global, may negotiate expectations to govern their relations with each other in carrying out policy *campaigns*. Alliances among indigenous groups, national NGOs, and international advocacy NGOs to challenge the construction of large dams such as the Narmada project have built expectations that govern international campaigns.[14] Or *cross-sector partnerships* can organize actors from different sectors—business, government, unions, environmentalists, and so on—to negotiate domain standards that enable collective action on shared problems by actors that might otherwise be in conflict. The World Commission on Dams, for example, brought together government officials, business leaders, civil society activists, and academics to jointly assess experience with large dams and to propose standards for future dam construction processes after it became clear that their ongoing conflicts were producing mutually destructive stalemates.[15] Such multiorganization domains can solve problems that single organizations cannot—but they can also create complicated legitimacy and accountability challenges.

When domain standards have not yet been established and societal ideals leave open many possibilities, agencies may have to create their own legitimacy and accountability standards through *organizational strategic choice*.[16] Organizations often have considerable leeway in defining how accountable they will be to various stakeholders, particularly when their stakeholders vary in interests and power. Ambiguity about societal and domain standards allows space for CSO leaders to make strategic decisions about their degree of accountability to different stakeholders. Those choices have consequences, of course. Leaders cannot choose to ignore stakeholders without legal, moral, or prudential risks. Ignoring the expectations of donors and regulators, for example, can undermine a CSO's access to resources or its legal legitimacy. Ignoring the interests of clients and staff, on the other hand, can undercut the CSO's capacity to create social value. But CSOs often behave as if they had less choice than they could exercise if they gave systematic attention to their options.

In the absence of strategic choice, some stakeholders are likely to receive more attention than others. In the panoply of stakeholders that have claims on CSO accountability, large differences in formal power and resources separate wealthy donors, authoritative regulators, marginalized clients, essential allies, and senior and junior staff. It is common for CSOs to pay more attention to the claims of donors and government regulators than to those of marginalized clients or junior staff.[17] While this prioritization makes sense in some circumstances, without analysis of CSO missions and strategies it is not clear that favoring more powerful stakeholders always supports mission accomplishment.

From the point of view of CSO leaders, it is easier to influence organizational strategic choices than to negotiate multiorganization domain standards, and it is easier to influence domain standards than to shape societal ideals. This book focuses first on managing legitimacy and accountability challenges through organizational strategic choice, then on managing those challenges through domain negotiations.

The Centrality of CSO Values, Missions, and Strategies

The legitimacy of CSOs is closely tied to the central values and organizational missions that define their purposes and reasons for existence. While the claims of multiple stakeholders can create conflicting accountability claims, the nature of the CSO's mission and organizational purposes offers an important touchstone for responding to questions of legitimacy and accountability. CSOs that create social value by producing goods and services can claim legitimacy on the basis of their production quality and quantity. CSOs that create value by building capacities of marginalized groups for self-help can claim legitimacy on the basis of demonstrated new capabilities among their clients. CSOs that create value by fostering political empowerment and policy influence for their constituents can claim legitimacy on the basis of their political impacts.

A central concern for many CSOs is the creation of a *strategy* that guides their use of limited resources to accomplish their often ambitious goals and missions. CSO missions and strategies define the public value the CSOs will create and how they will create it. There are a variety of approaches to thinking about CSO strategies and missions.[18] "Stakeholder" perspectives, which take into account many actors who affect or are affected by organizational activities, are increasingly applied to many kinds of organizations, and they are particularly appropriate to the many constituencies concerned about CSO activities.[19] More specifically, the "strategic triangle" perspective is particularly useful for focusing the attention of CSO leaders on questions that must be examined in the course of strategic thinking about their activities.[20]

The strategic triangle focuses leaders' attention on three fundamental issues: (1) the public value the organization seeks to create, (2) the legitimacy and support it needs to survive, and (3) the operational capacity required to accomplish its mission. While each of these questions may be relatively simple to answer in itself, the challenge for CSO leaders is to craft strategies that ensure that value creation activities are consistent with expectations for legitimacy and support as well as being within the operational capacities of the agency and its partners. The importance of maintaining legitimacy and support is particularly central for organizations (including most CSOs) whose resources come from stakeholders (e.g., donors or governments) who are not necessarily the recipients of their value creation activities. But even businesses, which rely on customer payments to support their ongoing activities, are increasingly concerned about wider legitimacy and support that continues their "license to operate" in some markets.[21] Figure 1.2 presents these issues in the strategic triangle format. The triangle emphasizes the interdependence of the questions: choices at one point of the triangle have implications for the other two.

Different strategies for creating public value require different approaches to legitimacy and support and to operational capacity.[22] CSOs that create value by *providing services*, such as disaster relief and or health care, may focus considerable attention on getting donor support in emergencies and legitimacy with host governments. They will be concerned with operational capacity to move relief supplies in large quantities, often

Figure 1.2 Strategic Triangle

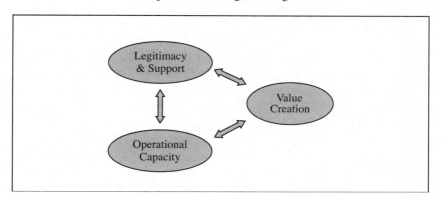

to remote settings, to provide basic services to large populations. Oxfam International, for example, moved thousands of winterized tents to victims of the Pakistan earthquake in 2005 to protect residents who had lost their homes at the beginning of the winter weather.

CSOs whose strategy emphasizes *capacity building* to enable client self-help, in contrast, often must enlist those clients in assessing needs, defining solutions, and implementing actions in order to co-produce new capacities that cannot be "injected" into passive recipients. When Oxfam builds "savings-led" microfinance programs to enhance rural women's incomes, it works closely with participants to ensure that programs are relevant and usable. So capacity building strategies can require legitimacy with, and accountability to, clients as well as funders and regulators, and operational capacities must be tailored to client needs to be effective.

CSOs that create value by *policy advocacy and institutional influence* face other questions. Political influence often depends on building legitimacy with political constituencies and target agencies. When Oxfam International advocates global policies to increase fairness in international cotton markets, for example, it builds alliances with developing country farmer organizations, international coffee corporations, and US policymakers crafting legislation on US cotton subsidies. This work requires operational capacities, such as access to media and Congressional lobbies, which are quite different from those of service-providing or capacity-building CSOs.

So CSO missions and strategies are central to defining their legitimacy and their accountabilities to various stakeholders, and strategic choices can have large impacts on the legitimacy and accountability challenges they face. CSOs that take on multiple strategies without thinking through the implications of strategic shifts can be blindsided by serious legitimacy and accountability problems down the road.

The Transnational Arena

There has been an explosion of interest in the transnational arena with the acceleration of globalization. It is increasingly clear that economic, political, and social problems cannot be solved by focusing on their local manifestations if they are caused by international institutions, policies, and events. The terms of international trade, for example, have much to say about the economic fate of Mexican small corn farmers deluged by "free trade" corn from large US farms or West African cotton farmers who have to compete with subsidized US cotton. Growing global interdependence has increased the availability of many goods worldwide—but it has also exacerbated the differences between the rich and the poor within and across countries.

The growing importance of the transnational arena offers both opportunities and challenges to CSOs. The opportunities for influencing global governance and problem solving are unprecedented. Civil society actors are undertaking expanding roles in relief and development activities, in shaping global norms and expectations, in defining policies and practices of multinational corporations, and in influencing the projects and policies of intergovernmental institutions.[23] Transnational arenas offer opportunities for civil society actors to shape discourses and policies that affect millions of people.

At the same time, transnational activity poses special challenges to establishing the credibility of civil society actors. At the transnational level, for example, there are fewer widely accepted values, norms, or laws that set legitimacy and accountability expectations. In transnational contexts, there are few institutions that can make authoritative decisions to set accountability standards or resolve disputes. Many emerging transnational problems are poorly understood, important to very diverse stakeholders, and subject to polarization and extreme power differences. Existing institutions are often ill- adapted or otherwise inadequate to deal with these problems. In order to operate in transnational contexts, CSOs must organize for cohesive action across regions and nations as well as across local, national, and transnational levels.

Civil society organizations that seek to establish their legitimacy and accountability in the transnational arena must deal with the loose organization of the arena, the emergent and highly charged nature of its problems, the inadequacies of existing transnational institutions and the vagaries of multicountry, multilevel, and often multisector organizations. This topic will be discussed in more detail in Chapter 2.

The Argument in Brief

Given the increasing importance of the issues, what can CSOs and networks—particularly those that operate in the transnational arena—do to respond to credibility challenges? This section overviews the argument put forth in the rest of the book.

In this book, it is argued that CSOs can *actively construct legitimacy arguments and accountability systems* rather than wait passively for governments and other regulators to set and enforce standards. Organizations can make strategic choices that enhance their own legitimacy and accountability; multiorganization domains, such as campaign coalitions, sector associations, or cross-sectoral partnerships, can negotiate expectations and agreements that define legitimacy and accountability for their members. While societal ideals are usually beyond the immediate reach of CSOs and their leaders, their activities often contribute to the maintenance or change of such ideals. Strategic choices and domain negotiations are particularly important sources in arenas that are poorly understood or lack credible sources of authoritative decisions, such as transnational governance and problem solving.

CSOs can *enhance their legitimacy* by justifying their existence and activity on several bases. Potential bases for legitimacy include compliance with regulations, association with other legitimate actors, demonstrated performance and expertise, political representation of constituents, embodiment of key values and norms, and close fit with widely held cognitive expectations. Legitimacy can be enhanced by complying with existing standards, informing stakeholders about that compliance, associating with practices and actors who confer legitimacy, and constructing new standards to fit the CSO's mission and activity. But legitimacy is sufficiently general and diffused among a wide range of stakeholders that direct enhancement is very difficult. For many CSOs, building accountability systems that enable specific stakeholders to hold the organization accountable to its mission and values may be the most efficient approach for enhancing legitimacy.

Constructing accountability systems allows framing the problem in more specific terms, so that legitimacy is generated by living up to the expectations negotiated with key stakeholders. Assessing existing accountabilities involves clarifying organization goals and strategies, identifying and prioritizing stakeholders, assessing accountability problems, and articulating visions for the future. Constructing accountability systems focuses on utilizing appropriate accountability models and mechanisms and carrying out a sequence of steps that defines stakeholders, negotiates indicators, enables performance consequences, and builds organizational support systems. CSOs can construct accountability systems that align accountabilities to key stakeholders with mission accomplishment. Organizational accountability systems are potentially useful for improving operational capacity and expanding strategic value creation as well as for enhancing legitimacy and support—though such synergies require considerable attention from CSO leaders.

At the domain level, accountability systems can enhance the ability of multiorganization communities to deal with legitimacy and accountability challenges as well. An early step in many domains is building an awareness of domain interdependence that outweighs members' resistance to investing in collective action. Building domain legitimacy can draw on similar bases and legitimacy management strategies. But for domains, as for organizations, creating domain accountability systems may be the most efficient response to legitimacy challenges. Domain accountability systems can draw on the experiences and analyses of multiple organizations and so construct standards and expectations within the domain that are similar to the widely held norms and regulatory rules that characterize societal ideals. This process of constructing norms and expectations may be particularly critical at the transnational level, where authoritative decisions are not easily created given the lack of agreement on governance mechanisms.

The argument distinguishes two perspectives on the creation of legitimacy and accountability standards. In some cases legitimacy and accountability expectations are created by *administrative decisions,* in which expertise and authority combine to set standards that are widely accepted. In other cases, legitimacy and accountability standards emerge from the clash of arguments and perspectives in discourses that combine past perspectives, emerging arguments, and the power and influence resources of participants in *social and political construction processes* that produce understandings, values, standards, and rules. In the transnational arena, where existing institutions and authorities are often unable to cope with emerging problems and challenges by administrative decisions, social and political construction processes are central to dealing with the challenges of globalization and increasing interdependence.

The Organization of This Book

Chapter 2 discusses the *characteristics of the transnational arena* that make legitimacy and accountability for civil society actors complex—and difficult to establish. It discusses the characteristics of the transnational arena as a loosely organized context with few accepted authorities, shifting sectoral roles, and dominance by elites with little sensitivity to many global problems. It suggests that emerging transnational problems are often poorly understood, largely invisible until reframed, and particularly burdensome to poor groups. The combination of loosely organized context and difficult problems is compounded by the widespread failure of existing global institutions to deal with emerging problems because of bureaucratic organizations, democratic deficits, and failure to meet good governance standards. Finally, civil society legitimacy and accountability in the transnational arena are undermined by the organization and management challenges facing transnational CSOs.

Chapters 3 and 4 develop a framework for understanding civil society legitimacy and accountability and for enhancing legitimacy and constructing accountability systems. Chapter 3 focuses on *assessing* legitimacy and accountability, discussing the concepts and their underlying elements. The chapter outlines steps in identifying goals and strategies, mapping stakeholders, assessing legitimacy and accountability demands, and articulating visions of desired future states that can justify the effort and expense of enhancing legitimacy or constructing accountability systems.

Chapter 4 emphasizes *enhancing* legitimacy and accountability. It examines the processes of social and political construction in complex and unregulated contexts. It describes possibilities for enhancing legitimacy in terms of various legitimacy bases and resources and different management strategies. It also discusses the construction of accountability systems in terms of different underlying models and mechanisms. The chapter also describes steps for constructing accountability systems by negotiating stakeholder expectations, assessing and communicating performance results, enabling performance consequences, and creating organizational implementation arrangement to sustain the accountability system.

Chapter 5 discusses *organizational strategic choice* as a vehicle for enhancing civil society legitimacy and accountability. The chapter draws on the experience of Oxfam International as a transnational civil society actor involved in international humanitarian assistance, grassroots development projects with local partners, and global policy advocacy in collaboration with its family members and many other actors to illustrate the issues in assessing and enhancing the legitimacy and accountability of a transnational organization. The chapter deals with assessing the organization's legitimacy and accountability, action to enhance its legitimacy, and interventions to build its accountability system. Finally it explores the uses of that accountability system in enhancing organizational strategy, capacity, and legitimacy.

Chapters 6, 7, and 8 provide a similar analysis for enhancing the legitimacy and accountability of three different kinds of domain. Chapter 6 focuses on the *civil society sector* as a common form of multiorganization domain. It illustrates the issues in the recent case of an association of international advocacy NGOs concerned with strengthening their legitimacy and accountability in the face of attacks by targets of their advocacy activities. Enhancing legitimacy and accountability in a sector domain involves recognizing sector interdependencies and dealing with histories of competition over funding and services that can undermine sector cooperation.

Chapter 7 examines the domain challenges for *multiorganization campaigns* to influence transnational policy making and problem solving. It illustrates the problems and possibilities with the example of an alliance across local, regional, national, and international civil society actors to stop construction of a thermal power plant in the Philippines. Transnational campaign alliances must often deal with differences in perspectives and interests across local, national, and global levels as well as differences across national bases.

Chapter 8 extends the analysis to the legitimacy and accountability of transnational *cross-sector partnerships,* in which organizations from business and government work with CSOs to solve transnational problems that no sector working alone can resolve. It uses the example of the Kimberly Process, which brought together CSOs, national governments, intergovernmental organizations, and transnational corporations to regulate the trade in "conflict diamonds." Cross-sector partnerships seek to solve intransigent problems by working across institutional sectors as well as across nations and levels of analysis. While they face very difficult problems of legitimacy and accountability both within the partnership and with external stakeholders, they are also a rapidly growing phenomenon for dealing with complex transnational problems.

Finally, Chapter 9 steps back from the details of enhancing credibility in organizations and domains to explore the larger implications of such initiatives. While the specifics of particular initiatives are central to their participants, it also appears that legitimacy and accountability struggles have consequences beyond the boundaries of particular issues. Transnational discourses about accountability and legitimacy interact with actions and resources of participants to construct new transnational values, standards and expectations for the parties—but they may also reshape the processes and institutions for constructing future political and social expectations. Struggles over legitimacy and accountability of CSOs and domains in transnational contexts may transform those actors—but they may also transform the transnational contexts and how they are governed as well.

Notes

. 1. For detailed discussions of the nature of CSOs, see Edwards, Michael, *Civil Society* (Cambridge, UK: Polity Press, 2004); Cohen, J. L., and Arato, A., *Civil Society and Political Theory* (Cambridge, MA: MIT

Press, 1992); Keane, J., *Transnational Civil Society* (Cambridge, UK: Cambridge University Press, 2003); van Til, J., *Growing Civil Society: From Nonprofit Sector to Third Space* (Bloomington: Indiana University Press, 2000); and Tandon, Rajesh and Naidoo, Kumi, "The Promise of Civil Society," in *Civil Society at the Millennium*, ed. Kumi Naidoo (Bloomfield, CT: Kumarian Press, 1999): 1–66.

2. Mekata, Motoko, "Building Partnerships toward a Common Goal: Experiences of the International Campaign to Ban Landmines," in *The Third Force: The Rise of Transnational Civil Society*, ed. Ann Florini (Tokyo and Washington: Japan Center for International Exchange and Carnegie Endowment for International Peace, 2000): 143–176.

3. See http://dictionary.reference.com (retrieved 9/29/07), drawing on *Random House Unabridged Dictionary* (New York: Random House, 2006) and *American Heritage Dictionary of the English Language*, 4th edition (Boston: Houghton Mifflin, 2006).

4. Surveys across twenty countries suggest that civil society remains more trusted than government, business, and intergovernmental organizations, though there has been a decline in the trust accorded to all three sectors. See Globescan, "Trust in Institutions" (2006) at http://www.globescan.com/rf_ir_trust.htm (retrieved 1/5/07).

5. Brown, L. David and Jagadananda, *Civil Society Legitimacy and Accountability: Issues and Challenges* (Johannesburg: CIVICUS World Alliance for Citizen Participation, 2007).

6. See Frumkin, Peter, *On Being Nonprofit: A Conceptual and Policy Primer* (Cambridge, MA: Harvard University Press, 2002); Edwards, M., *NGO Rights and Responsibilities: A New Deal for Global Governance* (London: Foreign Policy Centre, 2000); Brown, L. D., and Moore, M. H., "Accountability, Strategy and International Nongovernmental Organizations," *Nonprofit and Voluntary Sector Quarterly* 30, no. 3 (2001): 569–587; and Ebrahim, A., "Accountability in Practice: Mechanisms for NGOs," *World Development*, 31, no. 3 (2003): 813–829.

7. Globescan, "Trust in Institutions" (2006).

8. See, for example, Fremont-Smith, M. R. and Kosaras, A., "Wrongdoing by Officers and Directors of Charities: A Survey of Press Reports 1995–2002," Hauser Center Working Paper No. 20, 2003; and Gibelman, M. and Gelman, S. R., "A Loss of Credibility: Patterns of Wrongdoing among Nongovernmental Organizations," *Voluntas*, 15, no. 4 (2004): 355–381.

9. See Fox, J. and Brown, L. D., *The Struggle for Accountability: NGOs, Social Movements, and the World Bank* (Cambridge, MA, MIT Press, 1998); and Jordan, L. and Tuijl, P. V., "Political Responsibility in Transnational NGO Advocacy," *World Development*, 28, no. 12 (2000): 2051–2065.

10. See Keohane, R., and Nye, J., "Introduction," in *Governance in a Globalizing World*, ed. J. S. Nye and J. D. Donohue (Washington, DC:

Brookings Institution, 2000): 1–41; and Brown, L. D., Khagram, S., Moore, M. H., and Frumkin, P., "Globalization, NGOs, and Multi-Sectoral Relations," in *Governance in a Globalizing World*, ed. J. Nye and J. Donohue (Washington, DC: Brookings Institution, 2000): 271–296.

11. For discussion of the transnational roles of CSOs, see Batliwala, S. and Brown, L. D., eds., *Transnational Civil Society: An Introduction* (Bloomfield, CT: Kumarian Press, 2006); Clark, J., ed., *Globalizing Civic Engagement: Civil Society and Transnational Action* (London: Earthscan, 2003); Florini, Ann, *The Third Force* (2000); and Khagram, S., Riker, J. and Sikkink, K., eds., *Restructuring World Politics* (Minneapolis: University of Minnesota Press, 2001).

12. The issue of civil society accountability has emerged as a critical problem for civil society in most of the more than fifty countries that have assessed civil society using the CIVICUS Civil Society Index. It has also been identified as centrally important in discussions with more than sixty national associations of CSOs. Heinrich, V. F., Mati, J. M. and Brown, L. David, "The Varying Contexts for Civil Society Accountability: Insights from a Global Analysis of Country-level Assessments," in V. F. Heinrich & L. Fioramonti, *Global Report on the State of Civil Society*, Bloomfield, CT: Kumarian Press.2008, 325–340.

13. See Gupta, S., and Krishnan N., V., "The Credibility Alliance and Indian Non-profits," *AccountAbility Forum*, 2 (2004): 58–69.

14. Fox, J. and Brown, L. D., *The Struggle for Accountability: NGOs, Social Movements, and the World Bank* (Cambridge, MA: MIT Press, 1998); and Khagram, Riker and Sikkink, *Restructuring World Politics* (2001).

15. Khagram, S., "An Innovative Experiment in Global Governance: The World Commission on Dams," in Thakyur, R., Cooper A. and English, J., eds., *International Commissions and the Power of Ideas* (Tokyo: UN University Press, 2005): 203–231.

16. Brown, L. D. and Moore, M. H., "Accountability, Strategy and International Nongovernmental Organizations," *Nonprofit and Voluntary Sector Quarterly*, 30, no. 3 (2001): 569–587.

17. Ebrahim, "Accountability in Practice" (2003).

18. For example, Bryson, J., *Strategic Planning for Public and Nonprofit Organizations: A Guide to Strengthening and Sustaining Organizational Achievement.* (San Francisco: Jossey-Bass, 1988).

19. See Freeman, R. E., *Strategic Management: A Stakeholder Approach* (Boston: Pitman, 1984); and Post, J. E., Preston, L. E. and Sachs, S., *Redefining the Corporation: Stakeholder Management and Organizational Wealth* (Stanford, CA: University of Stanford Press, 2002).

20. Moore, M., "Managing for Value: Organizational Strategy in For-profit, Nonprofit, and Governmental Organizations," *Nonprofit and Voluntary Sector Quarterly*, 29, no. 1, Supplement (2000): 183–204; and

Moore, M.H., *Creating Public Value: Strategic Management in Government* (Cambridge, MA: Harvard University Press, 1995).

21. See Post, Preston and Sachs, *Redefining the Corporation* (2002); Austin, J. E., *The Collaboration Challenge: How Nonprofits and Businesses Succeed through Strategic Alliances* (Boston: Harvard Business School, 2000); and Yankelovich, D., *Profit with Honor: The New Stage of Market Capitalism* (New Haven, CT: Yale University Press, 2006).

22. Brown and Moore, "Accountability, Strategy and International Nongovernmental Organizations" (2001).

23. See for examples: Fox and Brown, *The Struggle for Accountability* (1998); Johnson, D. A., "Confronting Corporate Power: Strategies and Phases of the Nestle Boycott," in L. Preston and J. Post, eds., *Research in Corporate Social Performance and Policy*, Vol. 8 (Greenwich, CT: JAI Press, 1986): 323–344; Keck, M. and Sikkink, K., *Activists Beyond Borders* (Ithaca, NY: Cornell University Press, 1998); Khagram, Riker and Sikkink, *Restructuring World Politics* (2001); and Lindenberg, M., and Bryant, C., *Going Global: Transforming Relief and Development NGOs* (Bloomfield, CT: Kumarian Press, 2001).

CHAPTER TWO

Transnational Legitimacy and Accountability Challenges

In recent decades, civil society organizations (CSOs) have played increasingly important roles in transnational problem solving and governance. Their grounding in values and social aspirations positions them to attend to transnational issues when government agencies must focus on their national constituencies and when business organizations are driven by market pressures. CSOs in an increasingly globalized world can focus resources and energy on building transnational institutions and solving transnational problems in ways that organizations from other sectors cannot.[1]

In the transnational arena, CSOs have identified transnational issues, provided humanitarian relief, fostered poverty alleviation across national boundaries, developed and monitored international norms and standards, campaigned for transnational policy reforms, and monitored and assessed results of transnational initiatives.[2] Environmental NGOs challenged the activities of transnational businesses and intergovernmental actors; the Landmines Campaign built wide support for a global ban on anti-personnel mines; Transparency International spearheaded the drive to limit corrupt business practices; human rights organizations pressed governments to free political prisoners; the women's movement reshaped norms and regulations governing violence against women; and economic justice coalitions have pressed the World Trade Organization (WTO) and other intergovernmental organizations to set fair terms of trade with the developing world.

Transnational arenas present special challenges for civil society claims to legitimacy and accountability. These challenges emerge in other contexts as well, but they are particularly acute in the transnational arena. At least four aspects of the transnational arena contribute to these challenges: (1) the nature of the transnational context as a loosely organized and rapidly changing arena; (2) the emergence of new transnational problems that are poorly understood and controversial; (3) the shortcomings of existing transnational institutions for dealing with emerging problems; and (4) the nature of CSOs and networks that carry out transnational work. These aspects will be considered briefly in the following sections to build a base for discussing transnational legitimacy and accountability in subsequent chapters.

The Changing Transnational Context

The transnational context has many actors and interests that seek to influence events. In contrast to most national societies, however, it has relatively few widely accepted institutional arrangements that enable and constrain the activities of those actors. Civil society actors are among the many agencies for whom there are relatively *few standards of transnational legitimacy or accountability*. Many transnational civil society actors see themselves as subject to national laws and widely held values in their home countries and in the other countries in which they work. For the most part, however, there are few genuinely transnational standards to which they can be held.[3]

In part this lack of standards is a consequence of the *lack of mechanisms for establishing transnational standards and expectations*. The transnational context has few established authorities that can create widely accepted laws and regulations, few mechanisms for articulating commonly held values and norms, and limited opportunities to construct widespread cognitive agreement on "ways things are done." So the kinds of institutions and expectations that regulate activity, set expectations, and provide standards for legitimacy and accountability in many nations or domains are less available and less easily constructed in transnational settings.

Developments in information technology, transportation, and other aspects of globalization have generated *increased awareness and interdependence across national boundaries*. The world is shrinking, and the barriers among nations have been "flattened" in terms of information exchange, physical proximity, and mutual influence.[4] The globalization of world trade, for example, has dramatically redistributed production activities, increased concentrations of wealth and power, and intensified tensions across culture and value differences. Globalization has expanded awareness and impact across national boundaries, often exacerbating tensions between rich and poor, between industrialized and developing countries, and across religious and ethnic differences. Increased interdependence has highlighted the challenges posed by the dearth of shared institutions and of the capacities to create them.

The transnational arena has become more widely recognized as a *source of problems that have significant local impacts*. Environmental problems such as acid rain, ozone holes, and climate change, for example, may be caused by activities beyond the boundaries of the affected countries. Health problems such as HIV/AIDS or SARS can easily become global pandemics given the ease of travel across national boundaries. The terms of international trade enrich groups in some countries and impoverish populations in others, such as the effect of industrial-country agricultural subsidies on the livelihoods of West African cotton farmers or Mexican corn growers. Increasing global interdependence increases the impacts of transnational affairs on local problems.

Historically, decisions about transnational governance have been treated as the province of intergovernmental negotiations, with decisions largely controlled by the economic, political, and military resources of powerful states. Globalization and world trade have, however, altered the roles of governments, businesses, and civil society actors in transnational governance. Opinions vary as to how much international decisions rest on the coercive force of economic and military power or how much they can be influenced by values, norms, and "soft power."[5] There is growing agreement, however, *that business and civil society have exerted increased influence* on many transnational decisions over the last several decades.[6] The expansion of the roles of transnational civil society and business actors has provoked increased attention to their legitimacy as transnational actors and their accountability in using their influence.

Large and powerful actors—governments of large countries, transnational corporations, intergovernmental agencies—can make their interests known in transnational decision making, but *many groups have little voice in transnational policies*. Civil society actors have helped identify problems and enable voices to be raised for unheard constituencies on a number of international issues. For example, some civil society actors have helped amplify the voices of scientists and grassroots groups concerned with the destructive impacts of environmental policies and practices.[7] Others have shown how the failure to control the distribution and marketing of "conflict diamonds" fosters endless conflict and interminable "independence struggles" in some African countries.[8] Problems of political voice have drawn many civil society actors to engage in transnational campaigns—and have created intense debates about their legitimacy and accountability in the process.[9]

The transnational context is a loosely organized, rapidly changing arena characterized by large differences in wealth, power, and capacities for influencing international decisions. Legitimacy and accountability questions in the transnational context are shaped by the lack of institutions that define expectations or construct needed standards; the impacts of globalization on awareness, interdependence, and emerging transnational problems; and the changing roles of institutions and populations affected by globalization. From the vantage point of leaders of CSOs, one implication of the changing transnational context is the proliferation of opportunities for their organizations to catalyze innovations in response to new and urgent problems. A second is the increased need for civil society support for populations with little political voice or economic power, who are particularly likely to be victims of the growing global interdependence. Both social innovation and support for disadvantaged groups will be greatly influenced by how civil society leaders manage the special challenges of civil society legitimacy and accountability in the transnational context.

Emerging Transnational Issues

Work on transnational problems often involves understanding and influencing complex, ambiguous, and technical issues that are not yet *widely understood or even recognized as problems* by many actors. Better knowledge and understanding of the issue is a critical prerequisite to transnational action on many of them. The technical issues surrounding climate change and environmental protection, for example, have been subject to endless dispute, and much scientific work was required to build consensus on the issues before persuasive policy recommendations could be articulated.[10] For emerging transnational issues, sheer lack of information and understanding raises questions about who has legitimate standing to sound the alarm or propose solutions.

Other transnational issues remain invisible as problems until they are *reframed in terms that reveal their consequences.* Transnational action to control the trade in "conflict diamonds" from West Africa was possible only after analyses by CSOs indicated that some "liberation movements" in West Africa could be better understood as terrorists seeking to control diamond fields for their economic value.[11] When transnational problems are rendered invisible by geographic isolation or prevailing political interpretations, analysis by outside observers may be critical to seeing them as problems at all. Independent civil society actors seen as legitimate and trustworthy reporters can be central to reframing such controversial problems.

Some problems framed in local terms may reflect patterns and forces with wider significance. Recognizing the links across locally defined problems and *integrating local problems into a transnational synthesis* can be critical to catalyzing more effective action. The campaign on violence against women, for example, created a transnational campaign by integrating the common themes in movements focused on local forms of violence against women (bride burning in India, spousal abuse in the United States, political prisoner rape in Latin America, female genital mutilation in Africa).[12]

Framing issues in terms of transnational norms and values enables alliance building across countries and issues.

Debates on transnational issues are *often dominated by stakeholders with focused interests and extensive resources.* Multinational corporations, for example, exert much influence on discussions of world trade, since they have intense interests in the outcomes and resources for participating in debates. Less affluent and politically powerful constituencies, such as Malian cotton farmers affected by WTO policies or Mexican corn farmers affected by NAFTA, are often less aware or influential even when they are greatly affected by those policies. Marginalized groups are often poorly positioned to recognize emerging problems or to influence national and international decisions. Existing distributions of power and influence shape awareness of problems, consciousness of alternative solutions, and access to decision-making processes.[13]

Some transnational problem solutions require the information and resources of many actors. For civil society actors it is often easier to block problematic initiatives than launch positive transnational programs. Altering transnational institutional arrangements almost always requires more power and resources than civil society actors can mobilize by themselves, so *cross-sector alliances are often critical to transnational problem solving.* A treaty to ban landmines was not possible without active support from national movements and government allies.[14] Creating new standards for constructing large dams required joint inquiry by transnational corporations, intergovernmental agencies, technical experts, and transnational civil society actors in the World Commission on Dams.[15] Many transnational problems require cooperation with governments, intergovernmental agencies, or transnational corporations.

The complex, ambiguous, and contested character of many transnational problems poses significant challenges to transnational actors. The tasks of increasing technical understanding, testing political interpretations, synthesizing local versions of transnational issues, mobilizing marginalized stakeholders, and enabling intersectoral cooperation are all important to effective action on transnational problems. One implication for civil society legitimacy and accountability is the importance of knowledge and ideas in understanding and reframing problems in terms of existing values and discourses. A second is the notion of building wider alliances within civil society and across sectors to mobilize resources needed for effective solutions. A third implication is that the issues of legitimacy and accountability can be expected to emerge as critical debates, since many powerful actors have substantial interests in how problems are framed and resolved. Problem solving may require extensive negotiations and tests of strength across different interested stakeholders in order to negotiate solutions that utilize their resources effectively.

Shortcomings of Transnational Institutions

The rapid growth of transnational interdependence and the rise of transnational problems have taxed the capacities of existing transnational institutions for fair and timely decisions about complex international problems.[16] The transnational character of some problems—climate change; trade in arms; terrorism; trafficking in drugs, women, and children; trade in conflict diamonds; corruption—cannot be solved by existing institutional arrangements. Some existing institutions, such as the tradition of national sovereignty over internal affairs, actively hamper dealing with transnational problems. If national sovereignty as an institution protects activities that have devastating impacts outside national borders, it undermines the ability of the global community to protect itself.

Many transnational institutions have grown out of bitter experience with past failures of international problem solving, including the UN agencies and the Bretton Woods institutions (the World Bank and the IMF). But many of these institutions have been criticized as *ineffectual in dealing with current transnational problems*. They were created more than five decades ago to deal with the issues posed by a very different international context. They have been criticized as bureaucratized, elitist, and slow to adapt to the pace of global changes.[17] They are often highly politicized and seen as responsive primarily to the interests of wealthy and powerful member states rather than to the demands of emergent and rapidly changing problems.

Many of these institutions are *subject to "democracy deficits"* that make them unresponsive to popular concerns or subject to capture by powerful interests.[18] The World Trade Organization, for example, is strongly influenced by the governments of industrialized countries and by multinational corporations, often at the expense of the interests of labor, the environment, or developing countries. Existing international institutions are also subject to bureaucratization and elitism that make them unresponsive to local pressures. As a result, existing institutions are frequently perceived to be difficult to influence, resistant to innovation, and accountable primarily to rich and powerful stakeholders.

The emergence of new global problems and emerging threats to global public goods, such as climate change, has called for *creating new institutions designed to solve transnational problems* that are better suited to their special challenges. UN Conferences on varied issues (the environment, population, women's rights, social development) have identified issues and negotiated agreements on problem solving, though implementation has often lagged behind those expectations. Assessments of emerging problems suggest that new institutional arrangements will be critical in dealing with the growing challenges of transnational interdependence, scarcities, and other emerging problems.[19]

The World Bank has proposed four standards of good governance for developing countries: transparency, accountability, rule of law, and citizen voice.[20] It has also been suggested that *emerging institutions for global governance and problem solving should be encouraged to meet such standards*. Few transnational institutions meet these standards. Many forces operate to hamper transnational "good governance," from resistance by states that do not observe those standards internally or who prefer to preserve their freedom to act autonomously in the transnational arena to the technical challenges of meeting the governance standards in the transnational context. Many civil society actors, however, ground their international campaigns in efforts to enhance the quality of global governance, and the long-term project of improved governance can unite many diverse interests.[21]

The debate over transnational institutions is at the heart of constructing better solutions to the challenges of international governance and problem solving. Those institutions potentially contribute to building an international system that respects national members while it responds effectively to problems and to affected local constituencies by generally accepted standards of good governance. Civil society actors potentially have much to contribute to improving transnational governance— transparency, accountability, rule of law, and citizen voice are concepts that underpin many civil society campaigns. Civil society actors can help to hold existing international institutions to good governance practices as well as help to construct new institutions.[22] CSO leaders are increasingly recognizing, however, that if they are to be effective in constructing or holding transnational institutions accountable, they must attend to their own legitimacy and accountability as well.

Challenges of Organizing Transnationally

A fourth set of challenges has to do with organizing transnational CSOs to be effective across many boundaries while preserving their legitimacy and accountability. Work on transnational issues may require civil society organizations to grapple with issues of strategy and organizational form that allow them to coordinate programs and activities across national boundaries, societal levels, and multiple parties.

Civil society organizations have adopted a *variety of strategies* for work across national differences, as suggested in Chapter 1. Some provide humanitarian relief in cases of disaster, such as water, sanitation, and food to the victims of hurricanes or tsunamis. Others deliver services, such as health and education support, to otherwise underserved populations. Some emphasize capacity building for self-help with local groups and organizations to build sustainable improvements in their lives. Still others emphasize political influence and advocacy to reshape the activities of powerful government and business actors to the interest of their constituents. Large gulfs separate the diverse stakeholders of transnational organizations concerned with implementing different strategies and creating different public values. The choice of strategy shapes the kinds of legitimacy required and the nature of stakeholder accountability claims.

Transnational CSOs may also work *across many societal levels,* from local to national to transnational. Child sponsorship organizations, for example, mobilize resources in the industrialized countries to support service delivery and capacity-building initiatives at the village level in developing countries. So they must organize to work effectively with Northern donors as well as Southern villagers and with Northern and Southern government regulators.[23] Human rights CSOs work with local branches to identify and challenge rights violations at the national level while they also advocate for human rights norms and expectations at the transnational level, gradually building both transnational and national agreements on standards and national traditions of meeting them.[24] Coordinating across the chasms of interest and expectation that can separate local villages and international donors or policy makers may demand substantial organizational capacity and attention.

Transnational CSOs may take a *variety of organizational forms* to carry out different strategies and manage the challenges of coordination across countries and levels.[25] Some are international organizations with a shared hierarchy in which national branches report to a common leadership. They include unitary structures, such as PLAN International; centralized associations, such as Greenpeace International; and federations with strong secretariats, such as Amnesty International. These organizations are able to act relatively quickly and coherently in dealing with large institutions such as intergovernmental agencies or transnational corporations. Others are more loosely organized transnational networks or coalitions among like-minded but autonomous CSOs. Such networks include confederations, such as Oxfam International, or informal networks with even less central coordination, such as Social Watch. They provide more autonomy and independence to their organizational members, though they pay a price in their reduced ability to act quickly and cohesively in transnational campaigns. Still others are transnational social movements organized for collective action in different countries. Transnational movements are sometimes alliances of national campaigns such as the civil rights and women's movements. They may also be global movements focused from the start on international targets and strategies, such as the human rights and climate change movements.

There are often *close links between strategy and organization form.* Where the strategy turns on tailoring initiatives to fit local and national conditions, it may be important to foster local and national autonomy.[26] Where rapid adjustment to changing conditions across national and level differences is critical, more centralized organization may become important. Changes in strategy may call for shifts in organization. As Oxfam International, for example, has placed more emphasis on transnational advocacy campaigns to complement grassroots projects, its influence on national member strategies and tactics has grown. Organizational arrangements that are adapted to multiparty strategy and tactics are critical, but the emphasis on coordinated action across countries and levels can vary with different strategies.

Transnational CSO strategies and organizational forms both contribute to and are influenced by questions of their legitimacy and accountability. CSO leaders often find themselves pressed to consider the fit between organizational strategy and the organizational architecture adopted to carry it out. The remarkable diversity of organizational arrangements visible among transnational CSOs reflects the diversity of strategies adopted as well as the varied nature of the contexts and problems that confront them.[27] Mismatches between strategy and architecture, however, can affect CSO legitimacy and accountability, both directly in the eyes of key stakeholders and indirectly in impacts on performance. As pressures mount for enhanced legitimacy and accountability of transnational CSOs, leaders may face growing pressure to respond to perceived "best practices" in strategy and organization—a pressure that may encourage adoption of effective models, but also contribute to restricting needed innovations. Finally, work in the transnational arena often calls for multiorganization coalitions and alliances, which in turn demand that CSO leaders develop capacities for "bridging leadership" that enables effective work across organizations and sectors as well as national boundaries.

Creating Transnational Credibility

Constructing legitimacy and accountability for transnational civil society organizations poses challenges because of the special characteristics of the transnational context, the nature of transnational problems, the characteristics of existing transnational institutions, and civil society strategies and organizations. Those challenges have several implications for civil society leaders concerned with strengthening the legitimacy and accountability of organizations or multiorganization domains for the transnational arena.

First, this analysis suggests that *standards for legitimacy and accountability are contested and evolving for many issues and actors in the transnational arena.* The loosely organized transnational context, the shortcomings of existing international institutions, and the emergence of new transnational problems combine to make many of the existing legitimacy and account-ability standards irrelevant or inadequate. The evolution of legitimacy and accountability expectations will shape the processes and actors in transnational governance and problem solving in coming decades.

⌐ Second, *credible civil society organizations and domains may be positioned to play critical roles in transnational governance and problem solving.* Civil society actors have been central to many transnational initiatives on urgent social problems, including the antislavery, labor, human rights, disarmament, women's rights, and environmental movements.[28] CSOs as value-based organizations often are sensitive to transnational issues and their impacts on otherwise invisible stakeholders, whereas governments must respond to their national constituents, and businesses are focused on market per-formance. Civil society leaders often have learned to create value-based syntheses of issues that mobilize voluntary energy and interorganizational alliance building. The women's movement, for example, enhanced its international legitimacy by integrating under the concept of "violence against women" movements in many regions—burning brides for inade-quate dowries in India, female genital mutilation in many countries in Africa, rape of political prisoners in Latin America, spousal abuse in North America.[29] Framing a women's right to be free from violence required extending the traditional concept of human rights beyond protection from state action to include protection from private action by husbands and others. The transnational arena may offer special opportunities for civil society leaders concerned about particular problems.⌐

Third, neither the value homogeneity nor the acknowledged govern-mental authority that ratifies societal ideals at the national level is avail-able in the transnational arena. So *organizational strategic choice and domain negotiations are critical for creating transnational standards and expectations.* This is especially true for emerging issues and problems with polarized interests, where best practices or generally accepted solutions do not yet exist. Diverse initiatives across CSOs can generate innovative answers or improved understanding of problems, so encouraging different strategies is appropriate for many poorly understood problems. Domain negotia-tions across international boundaries, societal levels, and institutional sec-tors can span very diverse perspectives and resources as well as huge differences in social, economic, and political power. Civil society leaders who can build coalitions and alliances across such differences can catalyze large-scale changes and impacts.

Finally, it seems clear that as CSOs strengthen their legitimacy and accountability, *they enhance their capacities to challenge or cooperate with other transnational actors.* The dearth of accepted administrative author-ities in the transnational context makes social and political construc-tion processes particularly important for transnational governance and standard setting. Debates on civil society legitimacy and accountability often involve actors from other sectors. To the extent that CSOs create persuasive answers to legitimacy and accountability questions in the transnational arena, they enhance their own credibility and they contribute to shaping expectations of other actors in that arena as well. Multisectoral initiatives and confrontations on shared problems raise questions about the legitimacy and accountability of all the participants and how much they can or should make use of each other's resources in transnational governance and problem solving. As shared expectations and standards are negotiated, they increase the possibility of better understanding of the issues and more effective joint work across transnational differences.

Notes

1. For an analysis that focuses on the emerging transnational roles of civil society, see Kaldor, Mary, *Global Civil Society: An Answer to War* (Cambridge, UK: Polity Press, 2003). For examples of civil society's transnational activities see Batliwala, Srilatha and Brown, L. David, eds., *Transnational Civil Society: An Introduction* (Bloomfield, CT: Kumarian Press, 2006).

2. See Reinicke, W. and Deng, F., *Critical Choices: The United Nations, Networks and the Future of Global Governance* (Ottawa: International Development Research Centre, 2000); Khagram, S., Riker, J. and Sikkink., K., eds., *Restructuring World Politics* (Minneapolis: University of Minnesota Press, 2001); Fox, J. and Brown, L. D., *The Struggle for Accountability: NGOs, Social Movements, and the World Bank* (Cambridge, MA: MIT Press, 1998); and Florini, Ann, ed., *The Third Force: The Rise of Transnational Civil Society* (New York: Carnegie Endowment for International Peace and Tokyo: Japan Center for International Exchange, 2000).

3. Ruggie, J. G., "The Theory and Practice of Learning Networks: Corporate Social Responsibility and the Global Compact," *Journal of Corporate Citizenship*, 5 (2002): 27–36.

4. See Friedman, Thomas, *The World Is Flat* (New York: Farrar, Straus and Giroux, 2005); and Nye, Joseph S. and Donohue, John D., eds., *Governance in a Globalizing World* (Washington, DC: Brookings Institution, 2000).

5. Keohane, R. and Nye, J., "Introduction," in *Governance in a Globalizing World*, ed. J. S. Nye and J. D. Donohue (Washington, DC: Brookings Institution, 2000): 5–6.

6. Brown, L. D., Khagram, S., Moore, M. H. and Frumkin, P., "Globalization, NGOs, and Multi-Sectoral Relations," in *Governance in Globalizing World*, ed. J. Nye and J. Donohue (Washington: Brookings Institution, 2000): 271–296.

7. Social Learning Group, *Learning to Manage Global Environmental Risks*, Vol. 2 (Cambridge, MA: MIT Press, 2001); Keck, M. and Sikkink, K., *Activists Beyond Borders* (Ithaca, NY: Cornell University Press, 1998).

8. Smillie, Ian, "Not Accountable to Anyone? Collective Action and the Role of NGOs in the Campaign to Ban 'Blood Diamonds,'" in *Global Accountabilities: Participation, Pluralism and Public Ethics*, ed. Alnoor Ebrahim and Edwin Weisband (Cambridge, UK: Cambridge University Press, 2007): 112–130.

9. Florini, *The Third Force* (2000); Khagram, Riker and Sikkink, *Restructuring World Politics* (2001); Fox and Brown, *The Struggle for Accountability* (1998); Clark, *Worlds Apart* (2003); Reinicke and Deng, *Critical Choices* (2000).

10. See Social Learning Group, *Learning to Manage Global Environmental Risk* (2001); Victor, D. G., *Climate Change: Debating America's Policy Options* (New York: Council on Foreign Relations, 2004).

11. Smillie, "Not Accountable to Anyone?" (2007).

12. Keck and Sikkink, *Activists Beyond Borders* (1998).

13. See Gaventa, J. and Cornwall, A., "Power and Knowledge," in *Handbook of Action Research*, ed. P. Reason and H. Bradbury (London: Sage, 2001): 70–80.

14. Mekata, Motoko, "Building Partnerships toward a Common Goal: Experiences of the International Campaign to Ban Landmines," in *The Third Force*, ed. Ann Florini (Washington, DC: Carnegie Endowment for International Peace, 2000): 143–176.

15. Khagram, Sanjeev, "An Innovative Experiment in Global Governance: The World Commission on Dams," in *International Commissions and the Power of Ideas*, ed. Ramesh Thakyur, Andrew Cooper and John English (Tokyo: UN University Press, 2005): 203–231.

16. Rischard, J. F., *High Noon: Twenty Global Problems, Twenty Years to Solve Them* (New York: Basic Books, 2002); Reinicke and Deng, *Critical Choices* (2000).

17. Rischard, *High Noon* (2002); Reinicke and Deng, *Critical Choices* (2000); Fox and Brown, *The Struggle for Accountability* (1998).

18. Clark, John, *Worlds Apart: Civil Society and the Battle for Ethical Globalization* (Bloomfield, CT: Kumarian Press, 2003).

19. Rischard, *High Noon* (2002).

20. World Bank, *Governance and Development* (Washington, D.C.: World Bank, 1992).

21. Kaldor, *Global Civil Society* (2003); Clark, *Worlds Apart* (2003).

22. For examples of efforts to hold the World Bank accountable to its own policies, see Fox and Brown, *The Struggle for Accountability* (1998). For an example of civil society participation in institution building, see Maguire, Steve and Hardy, Cynthia, "The Emergence of New Global Institutions: A Discursive Perspective," *Organization Studies*, 27, no. 1 (2006): 7–29.

23. Lindenberg, Marc and Bryant, Coralie, *Going Global: Transforming Relief and Development NGOs* (Bloomfield, CT: Kumarian Press, 2001).

24. See Risse, T., "The Power of Norms vs. the Norms of Power: Transnational Civil Society and Human Rights," in *The Third Force*, ed. A. Florini (2001): 177–210 on "spirals" of interaction between national and transnational actors to create new human rights regimes within countries.

25. Many of the following examples are taken from Clark, J., ed., *Globalizing Civic Engagement: Civil Society and Transnational Action* (London: Earthscan, 2003). But see also Khagram, Riker and Sikkink, *Restructuring World Politics* (2001); Lindenberg and Bryant, *Going Global* (2001); and Young, D. R., 1992, "Organising Principles for International Advocacy Associations, *Voluntas*, 3, no. 1 (1992): 1–28.

26. Risse, "The Power of Norms vs. the Norms of Power" (2001).

27. See Clark, *Worlds Apart* (2003); Florini, *The Third Force* (2000); Lindenberg and Bryant, *Going Global* (2001).

28. For discussions of the roles of transnational civil society actors in these movements, see Batliwala and Brown, *Transnational Civil Society* (2006).

29. Keck and Sikkink, *Activists Beyond Borders* (1998).

CHAPTER THREE

Assessing Legitimacy and Accountability

In 1992 Transparency International (TI) was launched by an ex–World Bank official who took early retirement to campaign against the corrupt practices he saw as undermining development initiatives in many countries. TI was created to support reform efforts, but it soon became highly visible because of its Corruption Perceptions Index (CPI), which ranked countries on the basis of their perceived corruption by international audiences. The CPI rankings gained worldwide media attention, particularly in countries ranked high in corruption. TI became influential as national and international institutions, including the World Bank, sought to partner with its national reform alliances. At the same time, many looked for reasons to debunk TI's growing role. When one of the leaders of a national reform campaign was accused of bribing a fellow member of Parliament (to secure passage of an anti-corruption law), the resulting furor threatened to undermine the legitimacy of TI and its branches all over the world. [1] If TI itself practices corruption, how could it make a credible case against the corruption of others?

Credibility issues apply to many social actors. Questions have been raised about the legitimacy and accountability of businesses and government agencies as well as civil society organizations (CSOs), and for good reason. But the bases of legitimacy and accountability for business and government organizations are often more clearly established than those of civil society. Businesses owe primary accountability to their owners, and agencies of elected governments are primarily accountable to voters or their representatives.

The picture is less clear for CSOs. They are typically not "owned" in the same sense that businesses are, nor are their leaders in most cases "elected" by anyone. They are potentially subject to accountability claims by many different stakeholders, who may have quite different interests and so make diverse or even conflicting performance demands.[2] So generalizing to CSOs from the experience of business or government is a risky business. This chapter focuses on the special credibility challenges that are posed for CSOs. It begins with definitions of legitimacy and accountability as concepts and then provides a framework for assessing civil society legitimacy and accountability. Chapter 4 uses that framework to discuss enhancing legitimacy and constructing accountability systems.

Defining Key Concepts

The terms "legitimacy" and "accountability" have long and complex histories that will not be discussed in detail here. The focus here is on identifying definitions and attributes of the concepts that can be useful to leaders concerned with strengthening civil society legitimacy and accountability.

Legitimacy

The concept of *legitimacy* refers to perceptions by key stakeholders and wider publics that the existence, activities, and impacts of CSOs are justifiable and appropriate in terms of central social rules and regulations, values and norms, and widely held expectations. For example, Edwards has defined legitimacy as "the right to be and do something in society—a sense that an organization is lawful, admissible, and justified in its chosen course of action."[3] Legitimacy is lost or gained in the eyes of external observers who may differ considerably in their perceptions of a particular CSO.

Claims to legitimacy may be rooted in many different bases. The following list represents a synthesis of analyses of the legitimacy of both public and private organizations.[4] CSOs may ground their legitimacy on one or several of the six bases summarized in Box 3.1.

CSOs may gain *regulatory legitimacy* by conforming to rules, regulations and legislation that are relevant to their missions and activities. Meeting state standards for service delivery or procedures for organizational registration and reporting may create legitimacy for service or political CSOs. For Transparency International, a violation of regulations against corrupt practices could dramatically undermine its legitimacy as an anti-corruption agency.

Associational legitimacy comes from ties to highly regarded individuals and organizations. CSOs often recruit distinguished trustees as evidence of their legitimacy. Transparency International recruited well-respected leaders to direct its national alliances and to sit on its international board. Relief and capacity-building organizations such as Oxfam America and political networks such as the Campaign to Ban Landmines also strengthen their legitimacy by building alliances with respected organizations and recruiting distinguished board members.

CSOs develop *performance legitimacy* by providing resources, competence, and services that are highly valued by stakeholders. Plan International and

BOX 3.1
Bases for Civil Society Legitimacy

- *Regulatory legitimacy* is grounded in compliance with regulations and legal requirements.

- *Associational legitimacy* is created by ties to other actors or institutions widely recognized as legitimate.

- *Performance legitimacy* is based on demonstrated expertise, capacities, resources and services to stakeholders.

- *Political legitimacy* is rooted in representing the interests of members or constituents.

- *Normative legitimacy* grows from embodying and acting for widely held values and norms.

- *Cognitive legitimacy* comes from consistency with the expectations and concepts that shape how stakeholders understand the world.

Save the Children are recognized for expertise and resources for improving the lives of children. Transparency International provides information and expertise on corruption reform. The Landmines Campaign has valuable knowledge and expertise about policies that can contribute to reducing the havoc created by landmines.

The creation of *political legitimacy* depends on CSOs becoming credible representatives of the interests of their members or constituents. Political legitimacy is particularly central for CSOs involved in policy advocacy and political influence. The Landmines Campaign became much more influential as it became increasingly able to speak on behalf of strong national movements committed to banning landmines. Note that much of the criticism of advocacy CSOs as "unelected" and "unrepresentative" has assumed that political legitimacy is the only relevant form, though performance legitimacy and normative legitimacy are also important legitimacy bases for such initiatives.

CSOs build *normative legitimacy* by exemplifying widely held values and moral obligations, such as preserving human rights, protecting children, or working to increase transparent and responsive good governance. Plan International mobilizes resources from the general public by appealing to its concerns about impoverished children, and Transparency International's campaigns often invoke normative as well as performance bases for the legitimacy of national and international initiatives.

Mobilizing *cognitive legitimacy* for a CSO involves aligning its activities with widely accepted shared meanings and definitions that define "the way things are." Many CSOs adopt organizational forms and performance reporting arrangements to meet common expectations. Many CSOs struggle to keep their overhead costs very low because of the popular perception that low overhead percentages are generally associated with efficient performance—an expectation that can be very inaccurate, especially across organizations with different strategies and activities.

Different CSOs emphasize different bases or combinations of bases for their legitimacy. Most develop some degree of regulatory and normative legitimacy. Strategies that emphasize service delivery and capacity building often focus on performance legitimacy. Strategies that emphasize advocacy often focus on political legitimacy. Associational legitimacy is often particularly important to CSOs that are starting up or moving into new areas of activity. Cognitive legitimacy can be important to CSOs that work in areas where performance is otherwise difficult to assess, so that observers must use the fit between their activities and social expectations to evaluate them.

Legitimacy refers to the perceptions and expectations of the CSO in the eyes of stakeholders and the general public. Those perceptions and expectations are often quite difficult for CSOs to influence, since they emerge from forces—such as long-term reputations, media attention, and public response to CSO activities—that are outside the area of immediate CSO influence.

Accountability

The concept of *accountability* refers to a more specific responsibility to answer for performance expectations to particular stakeholders. It is most commonly understood as a relational issue in which the CSO is answerable to and held responsible by a stakeholder with a claim on its activity, though accountability can also refer to being answerable to one's ideals and commitments.[5] The focus here is on CSO accountability both to its mission and to stakeholders who affect or are affected by its activities. CSOs are accountable in relationship terms when they answer to key stakeholders for their performance promises.[6] Accountability is usually defined in terms of performance for a particular stakeholder, implemented through a process for assessing, reporting, and sanctioning that performance. But CSOs have multiple competing stakeholders, so accountability to missions may have to balance against or align the multiple claims of diverse stakeholders.

The articulation and enforcement of accountability claims with particular stakeholders depends on the model of accountability relations that underpins the relationship. Several models for the relationship have emerged from work in different sectors.[7] Different models imply differences in status of the parties, influence patterns among them, desired outcomes, patterns of information sharing, and bases for performance consequences. Organizations can use several models to guide their relations with diverse stakeholders. We focus on three such models here: (1) representative accountability, (2) principal-agent accountability, and (3) mutual accountability.

A commonly used model in government circles is *representative accountability*, which emphasizes the obligations of representatives to their constituents.[8] This model has roots in political theory and is often applied to public sector actors. The Confederation of Indigenous Nationalities of Ecuador (CONAIE), an alliance of indigenous people's organizations in Ecuador, for example, elects its leadership and can replace those leaders if they are not accountable to their members. To the extent that external stakeholders recognize the validity of representative accountability within CONAIE, the alliance gains political legitimacy. In representative accountability, violations of constituent mandates can lead to electing new leadership or other sanctions.[9]

In the business world the most widely used model is *principal-agent accountability*, which focuses on motivating agents to achieve the goals of their principals.[10] From this perspective, the major challenge is to design incentives that will keep the agent faithful to the principal's interests. Principal-agent accountability emphasizes the fiduciary responsibilities of agents and contractual definition of economic and legal incentives that encourage agents to act for their principals. Contractual obligations can be enforced in the legal system, and violations may result in financial or legal sanctions. When funders contract with CSOs to deliver services, for example, they may include provisions that require financial reporting and performance measures to make sure that the CSO delivers the services they promise.

A third model that is particularly relevant to CSOs focuses on creating *mutual accountability* compacts that bind members through shared values, aspirations, and relationships of social identity and trust.[11] The parties to mutual accountability define shared goals and "buy in" to responsibility for achieving them. Sanctions for violating expectations are social and relational, so relationships and trust become critical to implementing shared analyses and plans. Mutually accountable relationships depend on shared understanding, respect, trust, and mutual influence, and consequently may require more time and energy to create and maintain than contract negotiations or representative elections. The international alliances of civil society campaigns against World Bank projects and policies are held together by participants' commitments to shared aspirations

Table 3.1 Models of Accountability Relationships

	REPRESENTATIVE	PRINCIPAL-AGENT	MUTUAL
Status of Parties	Constituents most important	Principal most important	All parties important
Influence Relationship	Representative acts for constituent	Agent is subordinate to principal	Parties exert mutual influence
Desired Outcomes	Defined in general by constituents; specifics by representative	Defined primarily by principal; agent gets compensation	Defined by shared values and problem definitions
Transparency	Representative is open to constituents	Agent is open to principal	Parties are open to each other
Source of Incentives and Sanctions	Political support; media publicity; regulator oversight	Legal and economic sanctions; courts enforce contracts	Social and moral sanctions; peer networks enforce

and goals and by networks of trust and relationships rather than by economic contracts or political governance systems.[12]

Table 3.1 summarizes differences among these underlying models. CSOs use a variety of models of accountability in relations with different stakeholders: Donor relations often depend on principal-agent contracts; relations with members may be driven by representative mandates; and relations with allies may depend on mutual accountability grounded in histories of trust and cooperation. Using different models can create confusion, both among CSO staff who are not sure which criteria to apply and among stakeholders who have expectations that diverge from the CSO's. These issues make active discussion and negotiation of expectations an important aspect of using mixed models of accountability.

Relations constructed as one model may evolve over time into another. For example, a long-term relationship between a donor and a CSO may evolve from a principal-agent contract for specific outcomes to a mutually accountable compact to accomplish shared objectives grounded in a common analysis and mutual trust. When parties frame their relationship in terms of different models, serious problems can arise. Many CSOs from industrialized countries of the "global North" and developing countries of the "global South," for example, have used the language of mutual accountability in constructing "partnerships" for development projects. When Northern CSOs—sometimes under pressure from their own donors—invoke principal-agent concepts to administer partnership resources, their Southern colleagues who expect a more mutual relationship feel betrayed by the shift to a more asymmetrical and dependence-inducing model.[13]

CSOs often face complex combinations of stakeholders who have diverse expectations. CSOs that are *accountable to many stakeholders* may not be primarily accountable to any.[14] CSOs may owe accountability to donors who provide resources, to regulators responsible for their legal certification, to beneficiaries and clients who use their services, to allies who cooperate in programs and projects, to staff and volunteers who invest their talents and time, and/or to members who expect the CSO to serve their interests.

But it is often not obvious which of these claimants should take priority when their demands are not compatible. Without accountability to donors, funding sources may dry up; without accountability to regulators, charters may be revoked; without accountability to beneficiaries, services may not be used or useful; without accountability to staff and volunteers, operational capacity may be eroded; and without accountability to members and constituents, political credibility may be undermined. How tradeoffs are made among stakeholders in conflict, and who makes those tradeoffs, are critical issues.

The Interaction of Legitimacy and Accountability

Legitimacy is a more general aspect of organization credibility than accountability is, in that legitimacy reflects widespread perceptions across many societal actors and institutions. While institutional legitimacy is centrally important to the CSO's social role and ability to influence events, it is not easy for most CSOs to influence directly how others—particularly distant others—perceive their legitimacy. Changing the general perceptions of many diffuse stakeholders is a challenging task.

On the other hand, accountability refers to more specific and directly influenceable perceptions by particular stakeholders. It is possible to identify stakeholders and articulate indicators of performance and other expectations that they hold of the CSO. Explicit articulation and fulfillment of those accountabilities can enhance arguments for the legitimacy of the organization, even when it may be difficult to demonstrate the implications of its activities for all concerned stakeholders. In many circumstances, creating and implementing an effective accountability system is a good strategy for responding to legitimacy questions.

How do accountability standards become established? For some issues and problems there are well-developed principles and tools for assessing good practices and compliance with accepted standards. For example, there are variations in accepted financial accounting practices across countries and issues, but on the whole the standards for good accounting are pretty well established. In other areas there is less agreement on standards and practices. Emerging theories and practices of "rights-based development," for example, are generating a wide variety of new approaches to grassroots development and to new alliances among CSOs involved in what had been quite separate fields of development and human rights.[15] In areas where "best practices" have not yet emerged and wide-ranging experiments are important to social innovation, premature closure on accountability standards and practices may foreclose needed experimentation and development. So in part the existence of shared accountability standards reflects the state of a field's development.

An ongoing question in the evolution of legitimacy and accountability standards and expectations is the relationship between organizational strategic choice, domain negotiations, and societal ideals in developing widely held standards and expectations about good practice. The experience of Transparency International, for example, suggests that the strategic choices of one organization can have impacts on the negotiation of the standards of transnational domains for issues like corruption, and those domain standards may in turn shape societal ideals and legal expectations at the national and transnational levels. This issue will be examined in later chapters.

Assessing Civil Society Legitimacy and Accountability

Two rather different perspectives on the challenges of assessing civil society legitimacy and accountability have emerged in recent analyses.[16] The *administrative perspective* emphasizes analysis of legitimacy and accountability problems by authorities and experts who can identify solutions and best practices based on technical and scientific criteria. Underlying the administrative perspective are assumptions about the value of systematic investigation and rational choices that can produce the best possible set of standards and expectations. This perspective is reflected in the assessment of what has been called "rule-based accountability" in areas where expectations can be standardized and applied across a number of settings. Examples include accounting rules, formal personnel policies, and auditing standards.[17] This administrative perspective has dominated much of the earlier work on accountability and legitimacy.

The *constructionist perspective,* in contrast, emphasizes the analysis of legitimacy and accountability problems as a fundamentally contested process, in which actors with different analyses and interests struggle over the definitions of the problems involved, the desirability of different standards, and the nature of acceptable processes for establishing and enforcing them. The constructionist perspective assumes that many legitimacy and accountability problems involve implicit and subjective standards held by actors with diverse interests, expertise, and power. Agreements on legitimacy and accountability involve social and political construction processes that produce "negotiated accountabilities" that set criteria, measures, and interpretations of success that are tailored to the particular participants rather easily applied across many contexts.[18] A constructionist perspective is particularly appropriate to assessing complex performances, mutual accountabilities, and expectations that involve implicit, subjective, and negotiated standards. Note that negotiated accountabilities are particularly appropriate to changing circumstances that alter the needs of stakeholders or the requirements for achieving shared goals.

Leaders of CSOs that work in transnational contexts need some familiarity with both the administrative and constructionist perspectives on legitimacy and accountability. The administrative perspective and its emphasis on rule-based accountability can be important in understanding standardized "rule-based" expectations that have been defined by experts and authorities across many organizations. The constructionist perspective, on the other hand, is particularly important for understanding and setting expectations and opportunities in areas of contested interests, divergent perspectives, changing contexts, and ambiguous results. For such circumstances, too often "the rules do not apply" or CSO leaders must challenge expectations and standards that are inappropriate or actively harmful to the accomplishment of important values and goals.

Assessing the accountability of civil society actors is concerned with the general question "Who is accountable for what to whom and how?"[19] For circumstances in which the administrative perspective applies, the answers to those questions may be quite clear and straightforward. For other circumstances, the assessment process may be the start of political and social negotiations that construct new standards and expectations adapted to the special demands of the time and situation. Assessments that provide the bases for enhancing legitimacy and accountability involve at least five steps: (1) defining the focal actor; (2) articulating its mission, strategies, and goals; (3) mapping and prioritizing its stakeholders; (4) assessing its legitimacy and accountability challenges; and (5) articulating aspirations for a desired future with those challenges. Each of these steps is briefly discussed below. They will be described in more detail for organizations and domains in subsequent chapters.

Defining the Focal Actor

Answering the "Who?" question involves defining the focal organization or domain whose legitimacy and accountability is at issue. When the focal actor is an organization, for example, the boundaries between the organization and its stakeholders are usually quite clear to both organization members and external stakeholders. As Transparency International evolved from an informal network into an organization with a board and staff and offices, the boundaries between the organization and its external stakeholders—targets, donors, allies—became more clearly defined in the eyes of both organization members and external observers.

For interorganizational domains, on the other hand, the definition and boundaries of the domain may be ambiguous or contested. Initially there may be considerable ambiguity about who is in or out of the domain, or whether the domain exists as an important actor at all. Very often the nature and shape of its boundaries change as the domain evolves. As domains become better defined, potential members may choose to acknowledge and embrace their membership or to distance themselves from the domain. When the US child sponsorship NGOs began to discuss certifying members by a common set of standards, some NGOs decided to participate and others withdrew. The process may be even more visible in the creation of campaigns or cross-sector partnerships, where differences in perspectives and interests and histories may make potential members skeptical about the value of domain membership or joint action. But without some agreement about the definition of the domain, it is difficult to assess its legitimacy or accountability challenges.

Articulating Missions, Strategies, and Goals

Accountable "for what?" is a question that focuses attention on the missions, strategies, and goals of the focal actor—the value that the organization or domain seeks to create for its various stakeholders. Missions, strategies, and goals offer clues about the bases of the actor's legitimacy and the performance for which it might be held accountable.

For organizations, as suggested in the discussion of the strategic triangle in Chapter 1, the articulation of strategies involves attention to value the organization seeks to create (such as services delivered, capacities built, or policies influenced). It also requires leaders to think through how the CSO can gain and preserve external support and legitimacy for its work and how it will develop and maintain the operational capabilities required to carry out its strategy. CSOs vary considerably in how much attention they give to explicitly formulating their missions, strategies, and goals. But without such clarity it becomes very easy for

CSOs to drift on the turbulent waters of their social and political contexts or to become driven by the interests of powerful stakeholders, such as donors or governments.[20]

Articulating the missions, strategies, and goals of multiorganization domains may be more difficult. Getting agreement across organizations on what they seek to accomplish together may be quite challenging, particularly if there is a history of competition or conflict among them. For many domains, it is easier to organize the domain to respond to a common threat than to identify and achieve shared goals. Articulating domain missions and strategies is often complicated by membership changes as the issues and challenges facing the domain evolve. Policy advocacy campaigns, for example, may change membership composition over time and when advocacy strategies change. But some agreement about what the sector seeks to accomplish, what the campaign hopes to do, or what problems a cross-sector partnership expects to solve are critical to mapping stakeholders, identifying legitimacy challenges, and building shared aspirations.

Identifying goals and performance expectations can be straightforward or very complicated. For both organizations and domains, identifying goals requires becoming more specific about the public or social value to be created. More specifically, it may require articulating change theories or value chains that link shared activities to immediate outputs that are intended to alter outcomes for clients, partners, or beneficiaries and so contribute to long-term social impacts. Change theories demand that actors articulate desired futures, which can be difficult for both organizations and domains.

Mapping and Prioritizing Stakeholders

To the extent that accountability is a relational phenomenon, it is important to identify stakeholders who have accountability claims on the focal actor. The accountability "to whom?" question is commonly answered by identifying the stakeholders who have primary claims on the agency's performance. CSOs are often able to identify many stakeholders—donors, clients, allies, regulators, wider publics—with plausible and sometimes conflicting claims.

So a critical issue for CSOs is often balancing multiple stakeholder claims with the demands created by the organization's mission. Prioritizing stakeholder and mission claims can be challenging. Leaders can use at least three kinds of criteria to think about stakeholder accountability claims. *Legal criteria* are set by explicit regulations, as in the requirement that some CSOs publish audited accounts of their finances. *Moral criteria* are established by values and norms, as in the expectation that CSOs will serve rather than exploit vulnerable groups. *Prudential criteria* reflect the pragmatic consequences of failure to respond to stakeholder claims, such as the reductions in funding that might ensue after failure to respond to donor claims. Balancing legal, moral, and prudential criteria while setting priorities for responding to stakeholders and coordinating their domains with the requirements of missions and strategies is a critical task for CSO leaders. Different organizational strategies call for different priorities. The demands of good service delivery may require primary attention to service regulators and supporting donors, while capacity-building strategies require attention to clients who will co-produce capacity improvements, and advocacy strategies demand accountability to constituents or members as well as legitimacy with advocacy targets.

For multiorganization domains, stakeholder mapping distinguishes between internal stakeholders, such as the active members of the domain, and external stakeholders, such as domain donors, clients, or regulators. Accountability models and systems for stakeholders within the domain may be quite different from those employed with external stakeholders. Negotiating agreements on legal, moral, and prudential criteria for prioritizing domain stakeholder claims can be challenging when many diverse organizations are involved.

Assessing Legitimacy and Accountability Challenges

A first question is, What are the *current explicit challenges* to organization or domain credibility? Has the appropriateness or legitimacy of the CSO's activities been questioned in the media or challenged by important stakeholders? Are domain activities criticized by important publics or influential voices? Civil society actors depend on their reputations to mobilize resources and accomplish their missions, and explicit attacks on their legitimacy are necessarily matters of concern for their leaders. When two conservative think tanks organized a conference to discuss the legitimacy of the policy advocacy activities of "unelected" NGOs, they got the attention of advocacy NGO leaders all over the world. Explicit challenges by credible voices should attract leadership attention.

Challenges to accountability are often more specific and focused on activities subject to claims from a particular stakeholder. Media challenges to the performance of US child sponsorship organizations, for example, emphasized questions about their services to children and their use of donor contributions. Accountability challenges may come in terms of detailed critiques of how the organization or domain lives up to its own policies and standards of performance.

A second question in assessing legitimacy and accountability is, what are *potential future challenges?* CSOs can look at their missions and strategies to assess the kinds of challenges to legitimacy that might be mounted against them. The list of bases for legitimacy in Box 3.1 can be used to assess possible challenges to CSO missions, strategies, and activities. International advocacy NGOs, for example, can predict that they will be criticized as "unelected" representatives of constituents affected by targeted policies. Predicting future challenges allows leaders to prepare for them by enhancing their political legitimacy in representing those constituents or by clarifying other bases (such as the expertise of performance legitimacy or the linkages of associational legitimacy) that justify their roles and activities.

CSOs and domains can also assess potential accountability challenges, drawing on stakeholder prioritizations to identify potential problem areas. Table 3.1 can be used to clarify the accountability models that underlie their relations with key stakeholders and to think about the challenges that might be raised in the future. While assessing potential accountability challenges can absorb leadership time and resources, those costs may be more than repaid in the value of avoiding future challenges or having responses ready when they emerge.

Articulating Aspirations for the Future

The earlier steps of the assessment process provide a foundation on which leaders can identify aspirations and priorities for future work on credibility issues. How could the organization or the domain strengthen its legitimacy and accountability? And why would it want to? Compelling reasons may be needed to mobilize the leadership and resources required for such changes.

Some reasons may be rooted inside the organization or the domain. Strengthening legitimacy and accountability may enhance the organization's or domain's ability to create public value and build operational capacity as well as to increase its credibility with key stakeholders. The US child sponsorship NGOs took on the challenge of enhancing their accountability systems in part because those systems could be used for organizational learning and capacity building as well as for improving their legitimacy and accountability.

Other reasons for action may flow from relations with external stakeholders and forces. Threats to mission accomplishment may be averted, and new opportunities for strategic impact may be created, by enhanced legitimacy and accountability. The child sponsorship organizations believed that constructing a better domain accountability system would enhance their reputations with donor and media constituencies and enhance future financial support.

A common but often unrecognized source of pressure to enhance legitimacy or alter accountability systems is evolution in strategies of organizations and domains. As more CSOs add advocacy to their repertoire of strategies and activities, for example, their needs for legitimacy may expand to include new stakeholders (such as advocacy targets), and their accountability relationships may involve new stakeholders (such as represented constituents). So evolving strategies may have implications for relations with old and new stakeholders that are not obvious until leaders systematically assess the issues—or until explicit challenges to legitimacy and accountability emerge.

Enhancing legitimacy or constructing accountability systems can be expensive in terms of time, talent, and resources—especially of organization and domain leaders. So thoughtful assessments must consider not only aspirations for legitimacy and accountability systems for the future, but also the costs of creating and implementing them, the value of having those capacities in place, and the possible costs of being blindsided by future challenges. Articulating rationales for strengthening legitimacy and accountability is central to mobilizing the collective effort needed to carry them out effectively.

Summary

This chapter has focused on developing a framework for assessing civil society legitimacy and accountability. The concepts of legitimacy and accountability have been examined, and some of the underlying bases and models that undergird their operation in civil society contexts have been articulated. It is argued that civil society legitimacy and accountability

Figure 3.1 Assessing Legitimacy and Accountability

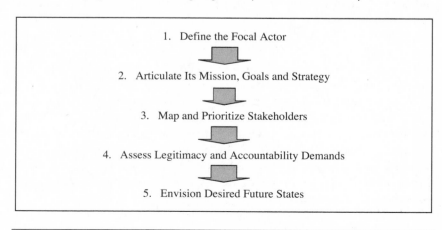

1. Define the Focal Actor

2. Articulate Its Mission, Goals and Strategy

3. Map and Prioritize Stakeholders

4. Assess Legitimacy and Accountability Demands

5. Envision Desired Future States

interact, and that negotiated domain standards and organizational strategic choices are particularly important sources of standards for civil society actors in the transnational arena.

A number of steps in assessing the legitimacy and accountability of organizations and domains have been laid out in this chapter; they are summarized in Figure 3.1. In practice, the flow is seldom as linear as this representation suggests because different elements interact with and influence each other. As missions and strategies evolve, for example, they can affect the definition of the focal actor or the nature of critical challenges. But for purposes of understanding the elements of assessing legitimacy and accountability, this rough ordering of the elements is useful.

Such assessments can provide the base for interventions to enhance civil society legitimacy and accountability. Enhancing legitimacy and constructing accountability systems is the subject of Chapter 4.

Notes

1. Information about Transparency International is taken from Galtung, F., "A Global Network to Curb Corruption: The Experience of Transparency International," in *The Third Force*, ed. Ann Florini (Tokyo: Japan Center for International Exchange and Washington: Carnegie Endowment for International Peace, 2001): 17–47.

2. See Cutt, James and Murray, Vic, *Accountability and Effectiveness Evaluation in Non-Profit Organizations* (London: Routledge, 2000); Frumkin, Peter, *On Being Nonprofit: A Conceptual and Policy Primer* (Cambridge, MA: Harvard University Press, 2002); and Goodin, Robert E., "Democratic Accountability: The Third Sector and All," Hauser Center for Nonprofit Organizations Working Paper No. 19, June 2003.

3. Edwards, Michael, *NGO Rights and Responsibilities: A New Deal for Global Governance* (London: The Foreign Policy Centre, 2000), 20.

4. This analysis draws on syntheses of the literature on legitimacy for private sector organizations by Suchman, M. C., "Managing Legitimacy: Strategic and Institutional Approaches," *Academy of Management Review*, 20, no. 3 (1995): 517–610; for public agencies by Brinkerhoff, D. W., "Organisational Legitimacy, Capacity and Capacity Development," European Centre for Development Policy Management Discussion Paper No. 58A, June 2005, 1–16; and for civil society actors by Brown, L. D. with David Cohen, Michael Edwards, Peter Eigen, Finn Heinrich, Nigel Martin, Mark Moore, Gabriel Murillo, Kumi Naidoo, Amara Pongsapich and Jan Aart Scholte, "Civil Society Legitimacy: A Discussion Guide," in *Practice-Research Engagement and Civil Society in a Globalizing World*, ed. L. D. Brown (Washington, DC: CIVICUS: World Alliance for Citizen Participation, 2001): 31–48; and Jacobs, Alex, Jepson, Paul and Nicholls, Alex, *Improving the Performance of Social*

Purpose Organizations: The Strategic Management of Organizational Legitimacy. (Cambridge, UK: Skoll Center for Social Entrepreneurship, 2006). For a discussion of the institutional aspects of legitimacy, see Scott, W.R., *Institutions and Organizations* (Thousand Oaks, CA: Sage, 1995): 45.

5. See Ebrahim, Alnoor, *NGOs and Organizational Change: Discourse, Reporting, and Learning* (Cambridge: Cambridge University Press, 2003); Fry, R., "Accountability in Organizational Life: Problem or Opportunity for Nonprofits?" *Nonprofit Management and Leadership,* 6, no. 2 (1995): 181–195; and Edwards, M. and Hulme, D., eds., *Making a Difference,* (London: Earthscan, 1992).

6. Brown, L. David and Moore, Mark H., "Accountability, Strategy and International Nongovernmental Organizations," *Nonprofit and Voluntary Sector Quarterly,* 30, no. 3 (2001): 569–587.

7. See Brown, L. D., "Multiparty Social Action and Mutual Accountability," in *Global Accountabilities: Participation, Pluralism and Public Ethics,* ed. Alnoor Ebrahim and Edwin Weisband (Cambridge, UK: Cambridge University Press, 2007): 89–111; Vangen, S. and Huxham, C., "Nurturing Collaborative Relations: Building Trust in Interorganizational Collaboration," *Journal of Applied Behavioral Science,* 39, no. 1 (2003): 5–31; and Goodin, "Democratic Accountability" (2003).

8. Behn, R., *Rethinking Democratic Accountability* (Washington, DC: Brookings Institution, 2001); Walker, P., "Understanding Accountability: Theoretical Models and their Implications for Social Service Organizations" *Social Policy and Administration,* 36, no. 1 (2002): 62–75; and Weber, E. P., *Bringing Society Back In: Grassroots Ecosystem Management, Accountability and Sustainable Communities* (Cambridge, MA: MIT Press, 2003).

9. Treakle, Kay, "Ecuador: Structural Adjustment and Indigenous Environmentalist Resistance," in *The Struggle for Accountability: The World Bank, NGOs, and Grassroots Movements,* ed. Jonathan Fox and L. David Brown (Cambridge, MA: MIT Press, 1998): 219–264.

10. Jensen, M. and Meckling, W., "Theory of the Firm: Managerial Behavior, Agency Costs, and Capital Structure," *Journal of Financial Economics,* 3 (1976): 305–360; see also Cutt and Murray, *Accountability and Effectiveness Evaluation in Non-Profit Organizations* (2000).

11. Behn, *Rethinking Democratic Accountability* (2001); Weber, *Bringing Society Back In* (2003); Ospina, Sonia, Diaz, William and O'Sullivan, James P., "Negotiating Accountability: Managerial Lessons from Identity-Based Nonprofit Organizations," *Nonprofit and Voluntary Sector Quarterly,* 31, no. 1 (2002): 5–31; and Ashman, D., "Strengthening North-South Partnerships for Sustainable Development," *Nonprofit and Voluntary Sector Quarterly,* 30, no. 1 (2001): 74–98.

12. Fox, Jonathan, and Brown, L. David, "Accountability within Transnational Coalitions," in *The Struggle for Accountability* (1998): 439–484.

13. See Ashman, "Strengthening North-South Partnerships" (2001).

14. See Frumkin, *On Being Nonprofit* (2002); and Brown, L. D., Moore, M. H. and Honan, J. P., "Building Strategic Accountability Systems for International NGOs" *AccountAbility Forum*, 1, no. 2 (2004): 31–43.

15. Nelson, Paul, and Dorsey, Ellen, "At the Nexus of Human Rights and Development: New Methods and Strategies of Global NGOs," *World Development*, 31, no. 12 (2003): 2013–2026.

16. See Weisband, E. and Ebrahim, A., "Introduction: Forging Global Accountabilities," in *Forging Global Accountabilities*, ed. A. Ebrahim and E. Weisband (Cambridge, UK: Cambridge University Press, 2007): 15–16; and Morrison, J. Bart and Salipante, Paul, "Governance for Broadened Accountability: Blending Deliberate and Emergent Strategizing," *Nonprofit and Voluntary Sector Quarterly*, 36, no. 22 (2007): 195–217.

17. Morrison and Salipante, "Governance for Broadened Accountability" (2007): 199.

18. Morrison and Salipante, "Governance for Broadened Accountability" (2007): 199.

19. Cutt and Murray, *Accountability and Effectiveness Evaluation in Non-Profit Organizations* (2000).

20. Moore, M., "Managing for Value: Organizational Strategy in For-profit, Nonprofit, and Governmental Organizations" *Nonprofit and Voluntary Sector Quarterly*, 29, no. 1, Supplement (2000):183–204; and Brown and Moore, "Accountability, Strategy and International Nongovernmental Organizations" (2001).

CHAPTER FOUR

Enhancing Legitimacy and Accountability

Some civil society leaders deal with credibility challenges as they emerge; others seek to prevent or minimize future problems by preemptively enhancing legitimacy and accountability. While early attention to strengthening legitimacy and accountability does not always forestall challenges, it does increase resources for dealing with them. This chapter complements the framework for assessing legitimacy and accountability in Chapter 3 with a framework for enhancing legitimacy and constructing accountability systems.

Chapter 3 discussed two perspectives on standard setting. The *administrative perspective* uses expertise and authoritative decisions to establish explicit and objective "rule-based accountabilities" that can be applied across many settings. The *constructionist perspective* uses ongoing discussions among diverse actors to build political and social agreements on "negotiated accountabilities" for complex, implicit, and subjective standards tailored to particular settings.[1] The administrative perspective is useful when compliance can be clearly and objectively assessed, as in financial accounting rules or fairness standards, and there is agreement on who will enforce standards across settings. The constructionist perspective is helpful when unambiguous and objective assessments are difficult, as in some kinds of performance or discretionary activities, or when no one is authorized to enforce standards across contexts.

Both perspectives are relevant to transnational legitimacy and accountability. For example, from the administrative perspective, an early achievement of Transparency International was catalyzing the creation and adoption of an Organisation for Economic Co-operation and Development (OECD) treaty that made corrupt business practices illegal in all the industrialized countries, so that corporations could no longer claim tax deductions for bribery in international contracting. The treaty created a new international rule to which corporations could be held accountable. Transparency International also found that sustainable impacts on corruption required tailoring reforms to the constellations of interests and issues that characterize particular industries. From the constructionist perspective, it has fostered sector initiatives, such as the Extractive

Industries Transparency Initiative to create standards for the oil and mining industries, and international public debates, with initiatives such as country rankings for perceived corruption and bribe paying, to build wider public support for reforms.

The most problematic credibility challenges often emerge when the standards involve diverse interests and perspectives, complex and poorly understood problems, and contested power and authority to set and enforce standards. These circumstances characterize many of the challenges to transnational civil society legitimacy and accountability, so the constructionist perspective is particularly important for civil society leaders in the transnational context.

The first section of this chapter discusses possibilities for politically and socially constructing legitimacy and accountability standards and expectations in the transnational context, drawing on analyses of recent standard-setting initiatives. The next section discusses enhancing civil society legitimacy, utilizing different bases and resources to develop legitimacy management possibilities. The third section explores the construction of civil society accountability systems that enable participation, evaluation, transparency, and performance sanctioning for different models of accountability relations. The fourth section explores the utilization of those accountability systems to improve value creation, operational capacity, legitimacy, and support. The chapter summary reviews key points and offers a flowchart for assessing and strengthening legitimacy and accountability.

Creating Social Expectations and Standards

Legitimacy and accountability have a dual character. On the one hand, civil society actors and their stakeholders have *subjective* views of their legitimacy and accountability. Those views may be similar, or they may be radically at variance with each other. Oxfam International and the US Trade Representative had very different views of the legitimacy of Oxfam's role in failed World Trade Organization (WTO) negotiations in Cancun in 2002. Oxfam thought its advocacy for a better deal for developing countries was highly appropriate; the US Trade Representative believed that Oxfam was interfering in discussions in which it had no legitimate standing.

On the other hand, in some circumstances there are relatively *objective* standards for legitimacy and accountability on which there is much more agreement. Explicit and objective standards for legitimacy have been defined for areas such as audits of financial accounts or board conflicts of interest for many CSOs in the US. It is relatively clear when those standards have been met and when they have not.

How do diverse subjective views evolve into more widely accepted objective standards? From the administrative perspective, research and theory identify "best practices" that are then promulgated as the objective standard by the appropriate authorities. This perspective is consistent with the idea that governments legislate to establish societal ideals on a variety of topics.

The constructionist perspective, in contrast, focuses on the emergence of new expectations and standards from a social and political construction process that is influenced by debates and negotiations over existing patterns and power distributions as well as by emerging arguments. For example, the expectations and standards that shape how corporations deal with environmental consequences of their activities have evolved dramatically over the last five decades through a series of debates and negotiations among government agencies, courts, environmental activists, and insurance companies as well as the corporations themselves.[2] Simon Zadek has argued that a central concern for organizational leaders in general, and business leaders in particular, is balancing organizational learning with societal learning, so the corporation adapts to evolving issues in the larger context.[3] Differences in standards and related actions create opportunities for debates and discourses that can reinforce existing expectations and standards—or redefine them. These debates can clarify the expectations of stakeholders, define criteria for assessing results, and set the stage for more widely understood definitions of both accountability and legitimacy.

Of course, agreement on standards is not inevitable in these debates. Civil society actors seldom have the power or resources to compel others to agree with their preferences, but they may have legitimacy with larger publics whose opinions count with decision makers. Elected governments are sensitive to the concerns of large voter blocs, and corporations are concerned about their reputations with consumers and regulators. Global surveys of public trust in institutions indicate that civil society organizations are often more trusted than either governments or corporations.[4] This credibility is a critical asset in dealing with other sectors. But the influence of civil society actors will decline steeply if their legitimacy is eroded, and credibility, once lost, is very difficult to regain.[5]

Debates and discourses about civil society credibility can construct and reconstruct expectations and standards. Compelling arguments about the inadequacy of current standards can influence debates and understanding of complex situations; those debates can produce new standards and expectations, which then shape future behaviors of organizations and domains. Those actions may in turn create new arguments and debates about expectations and standards.[6] For example, in the international regulation of persistent organic pollutants such as DDT or PCBs, the debate focused on whether the "sound science principle" (which requires demonstrated risk prior to regulation) should be replaced by the "precautionary principle" (which emphasizes potential risk in regulation decisions). The debate emerged out of an ongoing multisector, multinational struggle that culminated in increasing the emphasis on the precautionary principle in the new Stockholm Convention.[7] The constructionist perspective emphasizes the importance of building arguments from prior actions and framing them to challenge existing discourses in the negotiation of new standards and expectations.

Figure 4.1 summarizes the links among actions, arguments, debates and discourses, and standards and expectations in social and political construction processes. When actions grounded in existing standards and expectations produce problematic outcomes, they may catalyze new arguments in the debates and discourses that underpin future expectations. When Transparency International produces data about the corrosive effects of corruption on national and international development, it provides arguments for national and international debates about standards, expectations, and institutional arrangements that might reduce those effects.

As arguments become more compelling and powerful constituencies are mobilized in favor of alternative arrangements, the likelihood of negotiating new standards and expectations increases. Ultimately, new standards may be established by international agreements, such as the OECD treaty on corruption; by negotiated domain standards, such as the

Figure 4.1 Social and Political Construction

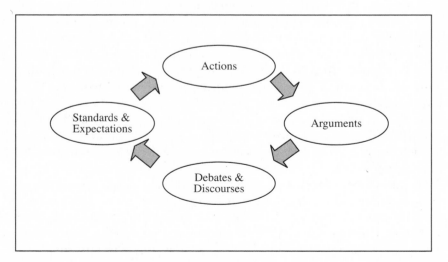

Extractive Industries Transparency Initiative standards; or by strategic choices, such as Transparency International's decision not to have political office holders in national leadership roles. At the transnational level, debates that develop widely accepted standards and expectations to govern international action are increasingly important for solving global problems. Since administrative imposition of standards and expectations through treaties or global institutions all too often fails to solve emerging transnational problems, some analysts have argued that the urgent need for better governance of global problems requires systematic use of discourses and debates across diverse perspectives to build new standards and institutions and the public will to implement them.[8]

Enhancing Legitimacy

Strengthening legitimacy may include developing better bases and more resources for demonstrating their validity. It may require managing those resources to demonstrate how the organization or domain fits existing standards and expectations or why new standards and expectations are more appropriate.

Legitimacy Bases and Resources

Clarifying which of the bases of legitimacy identified in Chapter 3 underlie the legitimacy of the organization or domain is central to coping with credibility challenges. It is not uncommon for challengers to emphasize bases of legitimacy that are not germane. For example, when the US Trade Representative challenged Oxfam International's legitimacy at the WTO negotiations as "unelected" by any national constituency, the charge was true—but irrelevant. Oxfam's claim to legitimacy in advising governments about WTO negotiations was based on performance legitimacy (expertise about trade negotiations and policy options) and normative legitimacy (supporting the value of "fairness" in trade negotiations with developing countries), not the political legitimacy of representing a national constituency. But responding to such challenges is difficult if leaders have not thought through the nature of their goals and their legitimacy claims.

Different bases for legitimacy imply different currencies and resources for their creation and maintenance. Clarifying the necessary bases for legitimacy can focus attention on how they can be enhanced. Table 4-1 summarizes bases for legitimacy and resources that may be used to develop and maintain them. Several kinds of resources are relevant to strengthening most legitimacy bases.[9]

Table 4.1 Legitimacy Bases and Resources

LEGITIMACY BASIS	GROWS FROM	LEGITIMATING RESOURCES
Regulatory	Compliance with legal and regulatory requirements	• Evidence of compliance
Associational	Connections to others widely seen to be legitimate	• Relevant knowledge • Recognized constituency • Cultural resonance • Longevity
Performance	Ability to meet the interests of stakeholders	• Relevant knowledge. • Demonstrable impact • Financial resources
Political	Represents an important constituency	• Recognized constituency • Demonstrable impact
Normative	Behavior fits and advances widely held values and norms	• Relevant knowledge • Demonstrable impact • Principled behavior
Cognitive	Behavior fits widely held conceptual categories on good practices	• Principled behavior • Cultural resonance • Longevity

Adapted from a framework created by Jacobs, Jepson and Nicholls; see Jacobs, Alex, Jepson, Paul and Nicholls, Alex, *Improving the Performance of Social Purpose Organizations: The Strategic Management of Organizational Legitimacy.* (Cambridge, UK: Skoll Center for Social Entrepreneurship, 2006).

Some resources for strengthening legitimacy can be quite concrete. When challenges raise issues of regulatory legitimacy, *evidence of compliance* with relevant laws and regulations can be vital. Tax returns and audited accounts, for example, can be used to demonstrate compliance with legal requirements. *Longevity* that is reflected in long histories of existence and acceptance may contribute to both cognitive and associational legitimacy. The possession of *relevant knowledge* or *financial resources* that enable contributions to stated missions and goals can often be clearly established as well. A relationship as a representative of a *recognized constituency* can also be established quite clearly.

Other resources may be more complex to establish, although they are important to legitimacy once established. *Demonstrable impacts,* for example, can be difficult to show unambiguously, particularly for actors involved in complex social problems. *Cultural resonance* may be critically important for establishing associational or cognitive legitimacy, but it can be difficult to pin down in concrete terms. *Principled behavior* can also be a powerful indicator, though establishing its presence requires opportunities to visibly resist temptations to behave in unprincipled ways.

As illustrated in Table 4-1, some resources are relevant to several kinds of legitimacy, while others are most relevant to a single base. For example, evidence of compliance with legal requirements is primarily relevant to regulatory legitimacy, and financial resources are primarily related to performance legitimacy. Relevant knowledge and demonstrable impact are each valuable for strengthening three bases. Cultural resonance, longevity, and principled behavior are useful for strengthening two. Leaders need to match resources to the most relevant legitimacy bases; for example, foundations with extensive financial resources and evidence of regulatory compliance cannot easily use these resources to build political and normative legitimacy.

Managing Legitimacy

Organization and domain legitimacy is derived from the perceptions of external observers and publics. These perceptions are often the product of complex interactions and forces that are well beyond the direct control of their objects. But analysts have identified at least four approaches to strengthening actor legitimacy.[10] The first three focus on aligning the CSO with existing legitimacy contexts. The fourth emphasizes constructing new definitions of legitimacy when existing standards and expectations prevent or constrain needed innovations.

Conform to Existing Legitimacy Standards

CSOs can comply with existing laws, regulations, codes, norms, and expectations that define legitimacy in their contexts. This approach can focus on any of the forms of legitimacy and utilize associated resources to conform to expectations. It is most useful when there are well-developed standards and expectation in the field and the CSO can provide evidence for meeting them. It is less helpful in circumstances that are novel or subject to few formal standards or widely accepted public values.

Meeting existing standards may be as straightforward as Oxfam International's publication of audited accounts and reports to donors on their activities. It may involve complying with the requirements for chartering or operating organizations in different countries. In some cases, particularly when regimes challenge civil society actors, compliance with regulations may undercut other kinds of legitimacy. When the government of Zimbabwe threatened to confiscate the resources of NGOs supporting human rights initiatives, the NGOs risked undermining their missions to comply with national regulations. Many left the country as a result.

Inform Publics about Current Legitimacy

In some cases, the issue may be lack of information or misunderstanding about how the organization or domain defines its legitimacy. CSOs can inform the wider public about how their activities reflect their missions and goals and so meet existing legitimacy standards and expectations. This approach emphasizes making more information available about the bases for legitimacy. The agency's access to legitimating resources may be part of the explanation of how it fulfills expectations. Building a "story" to explain the agency's activities can be critical to legitimacy strengthening.

Communicating with wider publics can be a complex and expensive process, particularly when CSO leaders are pressed to devote most of their resources to direct service and mission-relevant activity. When the US child sponsorship organizations were attacked by media stories that set unrealistic program expectations, they felt compelled to inform the wider public and their donor communities about how their programs operated to achieve their missions. When challengers threaten to establish unrealistic standards in the eyes of wider publics, CSO leaders take big risks if they do not act to create realistic expectations.

Associate with Legitimate Resources and Cultural Symbols

CSOs can use existing sources of credibility and cultural symbols to shape wider public perceptions of their legitimacy. Recruiting well-respected board members, adopting donor-approved monitoring and evaluation schemes, and instituting widely accepted organization structures and systems are ways to associate the agency with other sources of legitimacy. In some cases, these strategies may be largely cosmetic and have little impact on CSO functioning; in others, they may have substantial influence on organizational activity as well as on its legitimacy.

Building legitimacy through links to prestigious actors or symbols can also have its risks. Transparency International found that its ties to a high-level politician as the leader of a national reform branch made its reputation highly vulnerable when that leader was accused of corruption. But the recent success of celebrity awareness and fundraising in many industrialized countries for poverty alleviation illustrates some of the power of associating campaigns and causes with highly visible actors.

Construct New Definitions of Legitimacy

Aligning CSO activities with existing standards of legitimacy can reinforce the status quo the CSO seeks to change. It may be necessary to challenge existing laws, norms, cognitions, and interests to construct legitimacy consistent with desired innovations or social transformations. CSOs can reframe existing definitions to demonstrate their negative consequences and use their experience to articulate new understanding of legitimate goals. Constructing and reconstructing definitions of legitimacy may require catalyzing widespread public debate to articulate new arguments, engage existing discourses, and articulate new standards and expectations.

The construction of new definitions may involve intense struggles among competing interests. The struggle to reframe corruption as a legitimate problem rather than as an inevitable part of "the way things are" has required years of sophisticated multinational intervention by Transparency International and its partners. The effort to embed the "precautionary principle" in international institutions for regulating toxic wastes involved years of arguments and political contests to overcome resistance from many different interests. So reconstructing legitimacy standards and expectations of international publics is not to be undertaken lightly—but the history of transnational civil society activities is full of examples of reframing public expectations on controversial issues.[11]

These strategies move from aligning civil society actors with existing expectations to actively changing the expectations that underpin legitimacy judgments about them. Aligning a CSO with existing standards of legitimacy may be easier than constructing new standards, but for some CSOs, creating new standards lies at the heart of their development task—so struggling to transform present standards is vital.

Strengthening Accountability

Chapter 3 suggests that strengthening the accountability of civil society organizations and domains involves an assessment process that focuses on the accountability claims of specific stakeholders who are important to achieving organization and domain goals. That assessment can produce clearer aspirations for accountability to different stakeholders. This section focuses first on accountability models and mechanisms for building accountability systems and then on the steps involved in constructing those systems.

Models and Mechanisms

Different models of accountability relations imply different forms of organization and action as well as different underlying expectations. The systems by which citizens hold elected representatives accountable differ from those used by principals to hold agents accountable, and both differ from the ways in which partners in mutual accountability hold each other accountable. But accountability systems share some elements, even though they differ in underlying assumptions and goals.

Researchers and practitioners have identified a variety of tools and processes that can be used in building accountability systems. *Tools* are specific devices or techniques, such as audits or evaluation reports, that can be used for accountability purposes. *Processes* are more general and less time-bound mechanisms, such as stakeholder dialogues. Some accountability mechanisms combine processes with tools such as social auditing. The range of tools and processes available is increasing rapidly.[12]

At a more general level, these tools and processes serve important functions. The Global Accountabilities Project developed an elaborate definition of accountability for their studies of transnational business, government, and civil society organizations. Initial efforts to apply that definition raised questions that led to focusing on four functions deemed essential to fostering organizational accountability. Those functions can be accomplished by tailoring four kinds of mechanisms to the needs of the accountability relationship:[13]

1. *Transparency mechanisms,* which make relevant information about activities accessible, such as annual reports or public hearings.

2. *Participation mechanisms,* which enable engagement with key stakeholders, such as consultations about proposed programs with beneficiaries or oversight committees.

3. *Evaluation mechanisms,* which provide performance measures, such as evaluation reports or annual program review meetings.

4. *Complaints and redress mechanisms,* which enable response to stakeholder concerns, such as ombudsmen or independent evaluations of performance.

How these tools are employed may vary across underlying models of the accountability relationship. What is needed to enable transparency in a representative system may be quite different from the requirements for principal-agent or mutual accountability relations. Table 4-2 suggests some of the ways in which different models deal with transparency, participation, evaluation, and complaints/redress.

Leaders concerned with constructing accountability systems should be careful to choose mechanisms to fit the accountability relationships they seek to establish and implement. International NGO leaders have sometimes treated Southern NGO partners as agents when their relationships were originally constructed for mutual accountability and the latter

Table 4.2 Accountability Models and Mechanisms

	REPRESENTATIVE ACCOUNTABILITY	PRINCIPAL/AGENT ACCOUNTABILITY	MUTUAL ACCOUNTABILITY
Status of Parties	Constituents elect representatives	Principals contract with agents to act for them	Parties agree to achieve shared goals
Transparency	Representative reports to constituents on mandated goals; media assess activities	Agent reports to principal on contracted goals and activities; court investigates if necessary	Parties report to each other on compact-related goals and activities
Participation	Voters work with representative to articulate mandates and define priorities	Principal negotiates contract with agent to define goals and incentives	Parties influence each other to define shared values, goals and compacts
Evaluation	Voters, press, and oversight actors assess representative mandate performance	Principal and agent assess how each has lived up to contract	Parties and peers assess performances defined by compact agreement
Complaints/ Redress	Elections, media, and oversight actors enforce mandates with electoral and political sanctions	Courts adjudicate contract violations and enforce legal and economic sanctions	Peer networks enforce expectations with identity and reputation sanctions

have felt exploited and betrayed by that treatment.[14] International NGOs have also often assumed that installing a uniform accountability mechanisms across many countries will simplify work for their partners as well as for the international NGO—but that assumption is often wrong. Coordinating the expectations of parties to the accountability relationship can be critical to its efficacy.

Decisions about the underlying accountability model and how to handle transparency, participation, evaluation, and complaints/redress mechanisms are very important in constructing accountability systems. The process outlined below might be used in either an administrative or a constructionist process—but it has been developed on the assumption that construction is both more common and more challenging for strengthening the legitimacy of most transnational civil society organizations and domains.

Constructing Accountability Systems

Given limited organizational resources, how can civil society leaders construct accountability systems that are aligned so they increase the likelihood of accomplishing CSO missions rather than burdening them? The assessment described in Chapter 3 grappled with the first three questions in "Who is accountable to whom for what and how?" This section looks at the "and how?" part of the question.

Building accountability systems that provide the "How?" involves several tasks: (1) negotiating stakeholder expectations, (2) assessing and communicating results, (3) enabling performance consequences, and (4) institutionalizing the accountability system. These tasks are interrelated and not necessarily sequential. For different actors—such as CSOs, sector networks, campaign coalitions, or intersectoral problem domains—the emphases, resources, and problems to be solved may vary considerably.

Negotiating Stakeholder Expectations

How much attention should be paid to the accountability claims of the many stakeholders who affect or are affected by civil society initiatives? CSOs that do not explicitly grapple with defining, prioritizing, and negotiating stakeholder accountability claims often end up paying attention to stakeholders with loud voices and substantial power—such as donors and government agencies—rather than stakeholders with less clout—such as clients or agency staff—even when the latter are very important to achieving CSO missions and strategies.[15] Strategic choices about stakeholders and their claims may be even more important and challenging for interorganizational domains, which often operate in poorly defined, conflicted, and politicized environments.

Priorities for stakeholder accountability vary across activities. Service delivery CSOs may have to account to donors and service regulators to maintain the flow of resources needed to serve marginalized groups. Capacity-building CSOs may emphasize accountability to direct clients in order to co-produce enhanced capacity impacts for which client cooperation is essential. Advocacy CSOs may need to account to the constituents they represent and to build legitimacy with influence targets. Accountability to constituents is central to CSO legitimacy as a voice for unheard populations; legitimacy with targets may grow out of performance, normative, or regulatory bases as well as political representation by the CSO on behalf of its constituents. CSOs that undertake multifaceted strategies may have to adjust their accountabilities to many stakeholders as different strategies emerge as primary.

Defining and negotiating with stakeholders for multiorganization domains requires thinking through internal as well as external relationships. Members bring diverse interests to the domain and those interests may generate different domain goals and diverse relationships among internal and external stakeholders. Defining the domain's accountability to its members may be as challenging as defining and prioritizing its accountabilities to external stakeholders.

Setting expectations about performance can involve elaborate negotiations to align the aspirations of different stakeholders. Donors, for example, may expect assessments by indicators that are seen as irrelevant by CSOs; it is all too common for CSOs to collect one set of data demanded by donors and another set for their own learning purposes. Allies may bring different values and ideologies to campaigns and then feel betrayed by lack of consensus about performance and accountability on highly charged issues. For these reasons, explicit negotiations are often critical to aligning strategic priorities and the expectations of key stakeholders in a multiorganization domain.

Assessing and Communicating Results

Accountability systems depend on agreements about performance and how it can be measured. Measuring performance is particularly challenging when the agency seeks to accomplish long-term social impacts, since it is extremely difficult to measure such impacts or the contributions of various actors to them. Creating convincing "change theories" and developing indicators of performance that are plausible measures of success have drawn a lot of recent attention.[16] It is much easier to get unambiguous indicators of organizational activities and outputs, for example, than it is to measure changes in client or beneficiary behavior that is more causally distant from the CSO's activities. Even more difficult is unambiguous assessment of CSO roles in catalyzing long-term social impacts to which many actors have contributed.

Measurement challenges are also affected by CSO choices of general mission and strategy. CSOs that focus on disaster relief and service provision, for example, may find it easier to develop and measure performance than CSOs that emphasize local organization and capacity building or policy advocacy and influence. For all these actors, constructing indicators and criteria for assessing performance is important to enhancing their accountability for performance expectations.

The more general and ambiguous the expectations, the more difficult it is get clear indicators of success. Assessing and communicating results is particularly challenging for multiorganization domains that include diverse perspectives and interests. The challenges of assessing social and environmental impacts have received increasing attention in the last ten years. While many initiatives have examined ways to assess immediate outputs, others have paid attention to outcomes in terms of changed behavior on the part of program targets.[17] The work of organizations such as the New Economics Foundation, AccountAbility, the Global Reporting Initiative (GRI), and Keystone has expanded awareness of measures and standards for assessing social and environmental impacts.[18]

Enabling Performance Consequences

Since the capacities of CSO stakeholders vary a great deal, making the same information available to all of them does not ensure that they can all hold the CSO accountable. While government officials and donor agency staff may be happy with audited accounts or external evaluation reports, grassroots constituents may lack the languages (for example, English) or the skills (for example, accounting) to interpret them. They may also lack the resources to compel attention to their concerns even if they voice them. "Creating performance consequences" assumes some degree of voice and influence from all the important stakeholders, and balancing power among the stakeholders can be essential to ensure that the CSO listens to all those who are important to accomplishing its mission.

This problem is often recognized by CSOs—but less often solved. To the extent that development is understood as "empowering" grassroots constituents, creating the context for mutual assessment and joint learning with low-power stakeholders is an attractive goal—but not one that is easily accomplished. Accountability to clients and beneficiaries is an empty term if those groups do not have the power to demand attention to their concerns, but that power does not happen by accident. CSO experience with efforts to ensure participation with grassroots clients suggests that mutual learning and accountability has to be explicitly woven into programs and implemented with considerable commitment if it is to be effective.[19]

Institutionalizing Accountability Systems

Finally, enhancing accountability systems often requires the creation of new organizational arrangements, particularly when implementation demands significant resources. CSOs may create new roles or departments that can serve as resources for ongoing attention to accountability claims. Many CSOs have created evaluation and learning departments that mobilize organizational resources to assess programs and understand the perspectives of key external stakeholders.

The problem is more challenging in multiorganization domains, since it may require creating new organizations or delegating tasks to one or several members. Sector associations, campaign coalitions, and cross-sector partnerships are all organizational arrangements to support ongoing activity and accountability for multiorganization domains. *Sector associations* can develop codes of conduct for their members and use a variety of tools for monitoring and assessing compliance. Many associations ask their members to do self-assessments and then report on their compliance. *Issue alliances and coalitions* can provide interorganizational bases for accountability that involve long-term collaboration or short-term campaigns. *Cross-sector partnerships* can develop organizational arrangements that enable accountability across sectors and long-term governance of collective action even given histories of conflict among their members.

In short, the organizational arrangements for accountability systems vary widely across domains. This area has witnessed considerable ferment and development over the last decade, as more and more civil society organizations and their stakeholders have grappled with approaches to dealing with legitimacy and accountability questions.

Using Accountability Systems

How can CSO leaders justify investing always-scarce resources in constructing accountability systems for their organizations or domains? After all, everyone is more eager to hold others accountable than to be held accountable themselves. Why should sensible civil society leaders ask for trouble by creating mechanisms that their critics can use to create future embarrassment?

Chapter 1 suggested several reasons—some internal to the sector and others from the external context—why legitimacy and accountability have become important topics for CSOs. CSOs that build accountability systems can encourage better alignment of stakeholders with their missions and core values. They will be more sensitive and responsive to conflicting stakeholder demands and less vulnerable to unrecognized capture by the demands of powerful stakeholders. Those CSOs and their leaders will be less vulnerable to the general "crisis of governance" engulfing many organizations that have ignored accountability issues. Finally they will be better positioned to take advantage of the expanding opportunities for civil society influence on national and transnational stages that depend on continued and enhanced legitimacy and accountability.

From the contextual perspective, CSOs and domains that invest in accountability systems will be better positioned to respond to issues about governance and to questions about civil society misbehavior; they will be more prepared for challenges from advocacy targets and ideological opponents; and they can contribute more to improving public perceptions of civil society, setting the stage for wider influence and support in the future.

Figure 4.2 summarizes the links among CSO strategy, activities, results, and the accountability system. The strategic triangle attributes of value creation, legitimacy and support, and operational capacity on the left are central to assessing and developing accountability systems. CSO leaders must articulate strategies that integrate creation of public value with generation of authorization and support and development of operational capacity.[20] CSO activities to implement those strategies produce direct outputs (such as health services, capacity-building workshops, and policy analyses), outcomes in the form of changed behavior by targets (such as better nutrition practices by mothers, more self-help by villagers, and changed policies by legislators), and longer-term social impacts (such as healthier babies, improved quality of life in villages, and improved government services), as indicated by the large gray arrows.

Figure 4.2 Strategy, Accountability, and Legitimacy

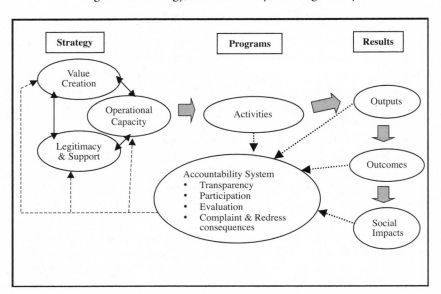

Learning and accountability are functions that are potentially syner-gistic but all too often separated or even mutually antagonistic.[21] Learn-ing and accountability systems are composed of transparency, participation, evaluation, and complaint and redress mechanisms that enable representative, agency, or mutual accountability relations. They use information about activities, outputs, outcomes, and impacts indi-cated by the dotted arrows in Figure 4.2. This information can be used to inform CSOs and relevant stakeholders for both organizational improve-ment and accountability purposes. Thus the dashed arrows from the accountability system to legitimacy and support, operational capability, and value creation reflect the use of performance information to enhance legitimacy, improve organizational capacity and performance management, and improve value creation.

Summary

Chapters 3 and 4 suggest approaches to assessing and strengthening legitimacy and accountability as resources for accomplishing the mis-sions, goals, and strategies of civil society organizations and domains. Figure 4.3 combines these discussions in a flowchart that summarizes the steps for strengthening legitimacy and accountability discussed in the two chapters.

Accountability systems potentially enable organizations and domains to negotiate stakeholder accountability demands that are aligned with their missions and so encourage them to live up to their performance promises. Such systems can help CSOs improve their operational capac-ity, adjust their strategies to create more public value, and build their legitimacy with stakeholders who support and authorize their work. Build-ing that legitimacy in turn positions them to play larger roles in the future, particularly as questions grow about the accountability and legiti-macy of other actors and sectors. Enhanced legitimacy and accountability can be critical ingredients in the future influence and roles of today's civil society organizations and domains. Perhaps more importantly, as indi-cated by the "domain and transnational impacts" at the bottom of the figure, the debates over legitimacy and accountability may well reshape domain and transnational discourses and debates, altering the way many stakeholders understand and act on the issues in question.

We turn in the next several chapters to application of this framework to civil society organizations and domains. Chapter 5 uses the framework to explore strengthening the credibility of a transnational CSO, drawing on the experience of Oxfam International as a case. Chapter 6 examines the challenges of strengthening credibility for a community of similar organi-zations, using the International Advocacy NGO Workshop as an example.

Figure 4.3 Assessing, Strengthening, and Using Legitimacy and Accountability

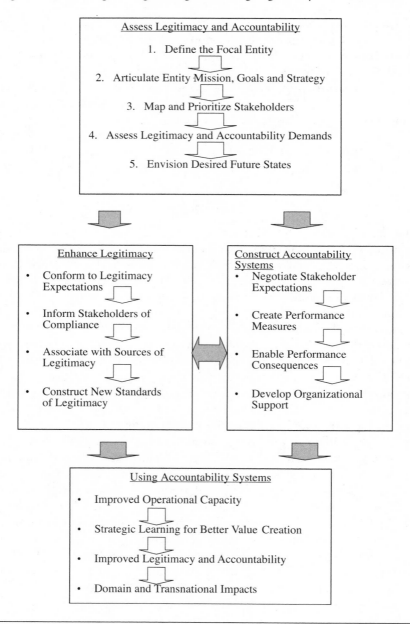

Chapter 7 applies the framework to a transnational civil society campaign to influence the World Bank and the Government of the Philippines. And Chapter 8 uses the framework to examine the evolution of legitimacy and accountability in a cross-sector partnership, drawing on the experience of the Kimberly Process to regulate conflict diamonds as an example.

Notes

1. See Weisband, E. and Ebrahim, A., "Introduction: Forging Global Accountabilities," in *Forging Global Accountabilities*, ed. A. Ebrahim and E. Weisband (Cambridge, UK: Cambridge University Press, 2007): 15–16; and Morrison, J. Bart, and Salipante, Paul, "Governance for Broadened Accountability: Blending Deliberate and Emergent Strategizing," *Nonprofit and Voluntary Sector Quarterly*, 36, no. 22 (2007): 195–217.

2. For a detailed description of the renegotiation of standards and expectations that have transformed corporate environmentalism, see Hoffman, Andrew, *From Heresy to Dogma: An Institutional History of Corporate Environmentalism* (Lexington, MA: New Lexington Press, 1997).

3. Zadek, Simon, "The Path to Corporate Responsibility," *Harvard Business Review*, December (2004): 1–8.

4. Surveys across twenty countries suggest that there has been a decline in the trust accorded to all three sectors—government, business, and civil society—but that the civil society remains more trusted that the other sectors. See Globescan, "Trust in Institutions" (2006) at http://www.globescan.com/rf_ir_trust.htm (retrieved 1/5/07).

5. Lewicki, R., "Trust, Trust Development and Trust Repair," in *The Handbook of Conflict Resolution*, ed. M. Deutsch and P. Coleman (San Francisco, CA: Jossey-Bass, 2007): 92–119.

6. For a general analysis of the development of new standards and institutions from debates and discourses, see Phillips, Nelson, Lawrence, Thomas B. and Hardy, Cynthia, "Discourse and Institutions," *Academy of Management Review*, 29, no. 4 (2004): 635–652. For a more specific application to the emergence of a new standard for governing international action on toxic wastes, see Maguire, Steve and Hardy, Cynthia, "The Emergence of New Global Institutions: A Discursive Perspective," *Organization Studies*, 27, no. 1 (2006): 7–29.

7. Maguire and Hardy, "Emergence of New Global Institutions" (2006).

8. Rischard, J. R., *High Noon: 20 Global Problems; 20 Years to Solve Them* (London: Basic Books, 2002); Ruggie, J., "The Theory and Practice of Learning Networks: Corporate Social Responsibility and the Global Compact," *Journal of Corporate Citizenship*, 5 (2002): 27–36.

9. Jacobs, Alex, Jepson, Paul and Nicholls, Alex, *Improving the*

Performance of Social Purpose Organizations: The Strategic Management of Organizational Legitimacy. (Cambridge, UK: Skoll Center for Social Entrepreneurship, 2006).

10. For treatments of the first three strategies, see Suchman, M. C., "Managing Legitimacy: Strategic and Institutional Approaches," *Academy of Management Review*, 20, no. 3 (1995): 517–610; and (for public agencies) Brinkerhoff, D. W., *Organisational Legitimacy, Capacity and Capacity Development* (Maastricht, Netherlands: European Centre for Development Policy Management, 2005): 1–16. The fourth strategy grows out of the special roles of some civil society organizations and networks as constructors of new norms and as managers of social meanings ; see Brown, L. David, and Jagadananda, "Civil Society Legitimacy and Accountability: Issues and Challenges" (Johannesburg: CIVICUS World Alliance for Citizen Participation, 2007). Also see Keck, Margaret and Sikkink, Kathryn, *Activists without Borders* (Ithaca, NY: Cornell University Press, 1998); and Khagram, Sanjeev, Riker, James and Sikkink, Kathryn, *Restructuring World Politics* (Minneapolis: University of Minnesota Press, 2001).

11. For examples of successful global campaigns on a number of issues, see Batliwala, Srilatha, and Brown, L. David, eds., *Transnational Civil Society: An Introduction* (Bloomfield, CT: Kumarian Press, 2006); and Keck and Sikkink, *Activists without Borders* (1998).

12. See Ebrahim, Alnoor, "Accountability in Practice: Mechanisms for NGOs," *World Developmment*, 31, no. 3 (2003): 813–829; and Blagescu, M., "What Makes Global Organisations Accountable? Reassessing the Global Accountability Framework," Working Paper 101, One World Trust, 2004.

13. Blagescu, "What Makes Global Organisations Accountable?" (2004).

14. See Ashman, Darcy, "Strengthening North-South Partnerships for Sustainable Development," *Nonprofit and Voluntary Sector Quarterly*, 30, no. 1 (2001): 74–98; and Leach, Mark W., "Organizing Images and the Structuring of Interorganizational Relations" (PhD dissertation, Boston University, 1995).

15. See Ebrahim, "Accountability in Practice" (2003); and Edwards, Michael and Hulme, David, *Beyond the Magic Bullet: NGO Performance and Accountability in the Post-Cold War World* (West Hartford, CT: Kumarian Press, 1996).

16. For tools to articulate social change theories, see materials on the Keystone Web site at http://www.keystonereporting.org/. For a manual for constructing logic models that articulate the sequences of outputs, outcomes, and impacts involved in social change activities, see the W. K. Kellogg Foundation Web site at http://www.wkkf.org/Pubs/Tools/Evaluation/Pub3669.pdf.

17. For work on assessment of development outcomes, see for

example Earl, S., Carden, F. and Smutylo, T., *Outcome Mapping: Building Learning and Reflection into Development Programs* (Ottawa: International Development and Research Centre, 2001); and Estrella, M., Blauert, J., Campilan, D., Gaventa, J., Gonsalves, J., Guijt, I., Johnson D., and Ricafort, R., *Learning from Change: Issues and Experiences in Participatory Monitoring and Evaluation* (London: Intermediate Technology Publications, 2000).

18. The Web site address for the New Economics Foundation is http://www.neweconomics.org/gen/; for AccountAbility, http://www.accountability21.net; for the Global Reporting Initiative http://www.globalreporting.org/Home and for Keystone, http://www.keystonereporting.org.

19. See ActionAid's Accountability, Learning, and Planning System (ALPS) at http://www.actionaid.org.uk/800/alps.html; for examples of efforts to ensure organizational learning from experience, see also Smillie, Ian, and Hailey, John, *Managing for Change: Leadership, Strategy and Management in Asian NGOs* (London: Earthscan, 2001).

20. Moore, M., "Managing for Value: Organizational Strategy in For-profit, Nonprofit, and Governmental Organizations," *Nonprofit and Voluntary Sector Quarterly*, 29, no. 1, Supplement (2000): 183–204; and Brown, L. David and Moore, Mark H., "Accountability, Strategy and International Nongovernmental Organizations," *Nonprofit and Voluntary Sector Quarterly*, 30, no. 3 (2001): 569–587.

21. For an interesting exploration of these tensions, see Ebrahim, Alnoor, "Accountability Myopia: Losing Sight of Organizational Learning," *Nonprofit and Voluntary Sector Quarterly*, 34, no. 1 (2005): 56–87.

CHAPTER FIVE

Strategic Choice and Organizational Credibility

Shaping the strategic choices of civil society organizations is perhaps the simplest way that civil society leaders can respond to credibility questions. While some transnational civil society organizaitons (CSOs) might argue they have little choice in the face of constraints posed by home and host country governments and eagle-eyed donors, many others have discovered considerable strategic flexibility in how the CSO frames its mission, what strategies it chooses to carry it out, and how it deals with the accountability claims of diverse stakeholders.

Organizational strategic choices are made in the context of widely shared societal ideals and negotiated domain standards that foster concepts of legitimacy and accountability. When societal ideals or domain standards have not yet been established—as is common in the transnational arena—organizational missions and strategic choices may be central sources of legitimacy and accountability standards.

For example, Oxfam International is a transnational CSO that combines work on disaster relief, support for projects to empower local partner organizations, and multileveled campaigns to influence global public policies on issues that affect poor and marginalized populations. It was created by a "family" of a dozen CSOs based in different Northern countries to enable better coordination of joint projects and improved policy campaigning as well as improved management of their shared stake in the Oxfam name. Oxfam International frequently grapples with questions of its own legitimacy and accountability, in part to respond to challenges from government agencies and corporations that have been the targets of its advocacy campaigns.

The touchstone for strengthening CSO credibility is the mission and values it seeks to promote and the strategies it uses to further them. To some extent CSOs are guided by clear objective rules and standards, such as legal charters and widely shared rules for good accounting practices. On other issues, however, CSOs and their stakeholders need to create negotiated accountabilities that are grounded in the specific circumstances and interests of the parties. Subjective differences about what makes the organization legitimate and accountable can lead to much debate. These debates potentially produce more widely shared understanding of an organization's identity and roles, more agreement about its legitimacy, and more specific expectations for accountabilities to different stakeholders.

This chapter focuses on managing credibility issues at the organizational level. The first section discusses the assessment of organizational legitimacy and accountability challenges. The second section examines the possibilities for enhancing organizational legitimacy directly, and the third section focuses on constructing organizational accountability systems that can align stakeholder accountabilities with mission accomplishment. The last section discusses using accountability systems to advance CSO mission accomplishment. The case of Oxfam International illustrates the issues of grappling with organizational legitimacy and accountability in a transnational context.

Assessing Legitimacy and Accountabilities

The framework proposed in Chapter 3 for assessing CSO legitimacy and accountabilities suggests attention to five issues: (1) defining the focal actor; (2) articulating its mission, goals, and strategy for creating public value; (3) mapping and prioritizing organizational stakeholders; (4) assessing current legitimacy and accountability challenges; and (5) articulating aspirations for the future. This assessment can then be the basis for enhancing legitimacy or constructing accountability systems that can be used for many purposes.

Defining the Focal Actor

When civil society leaders think about the strategic choices of a CSO, it seems obvious that the focus of attention is on that organization as a focal actor. What other focus would make sense? Are not organizations coherent social systems organized to coordinate their elements to achieve agreed goals and activities, united under organizational leaders to achieve their missions in efficient and effective ways?

Maybe. But maybe not. Organization theorists have explored a broad range of metaphors to explain the characteristics of CSOs, not all of which are as tightly organized or leader-centric as the description above.[1] Many civil society leaders have found that CSOs, in part dependent on the voluntary commitments of key staff, do not respond well to "command and control" models of organizations. Moreover, organizations engaged in producing innovative answers to complex problems may need to be loosely organized and nonbureaucratic to enable creative thinking and innovative and experimental action.[2] Strategic choices may involve a wide range of participants in some kinds of organizations on some kinds of issues.

The question about the focal actor can be particularly complex in transnational CSOs. CSOs that operate across many national boundaries have adopted organizational forms that vary from relatively centralized to radically decentralized, depending on the nature of their work and the challenges they face. Oxfam International, for example, is itself the creation of its members, designed to foster better coordination of relief and development programs and to enable more effective international policy advocacy. On some issues, its members would insist that they be the focal actors in strategic choices; on other issues they might insist that Oxfam International take the lead.

For the most part, defining the focal actor for organizational strategic choices *is* in fact a straightforward focus on the organization. It becomes more complex in the cases of multiorganization domains, in which agreements about the nature and composition of the domain may have to be constructed prior to the development of a clear mission or strategy.

Articulating Missions, Goals and Strategies

CSOs' missions, goals, and strategies define the public value that they seek to create and how they will create it, so they are central to defining legitimacy and accountability as well. Chapter 1 described the strategic triangle as a way for civil society leaders to focus attention on three fundamental issues: (1) the public value the organization seeks to create, (2) the legitimacy and support it needs to survive, and (3) the operational capacity required to accomplish its mission.[3]

Different strategies require different approaches to legitimacy and accountability.[4] CSOs that emphasize *disaster relief and services* for complex emergencies need access to large amounts of support, capacity to deliver good services, legitimacy with governments and international agencies, and capacity to move relief supplies in large quantities, often to remote settings. They may be particularly accountable to donors and regulators of their services. Oxfam International moved thousands of winterized tents to protect thousands of victims of the Pakistan earthquake in 2005 who had lost their homes at the beginning of winter. It also worked closely with local partners, who had ongoing relationships with some Oxfam members, to provide services focused on rehabilitation and renewal of devastated communities.

CSOs engaged in *capacity-building* strategies that enable client self-help, in contrast, must often engage those clients in assessing needs, defining solutions, planning action strategies, and implementing plans if they are to leave them with new capacities. Complex new capacities cannot for the most part be "injected" into passive recipients; they have to be co-produced by collaboration of the providers and recipients. When Oxfam works with local empowerment projects or local CSO partners to enhance emergency preparedness, partner participation in defining goals and assessing progress is central to effective capacity building. So it is necessary for a CSO to have legitimacy with, and accountability to, clients of the program as well as funders and regulators.

CSOs that use *policy-advocacy and institutional-influence* strategies face other questions about operational capacity or legitimacy and support. Influence and advocacy often depend on building relations with both political constituencies and target agencies. For example, when Oxfam International seeks to influence global policies in order to increase fairness in international cotton markets, it works to build support among developing-country cotton farmer alliances as well as legitimacy with policymakers in the US Congress (who write legislation like the 2007 Farm Bill that subsidizes US cotton production). This work also requires legitimacy with the media and alliances with US lobbyists concerned with the Farm Bill.

A key element of most CSO strategies is a *change theory* about how the organization's work will advance its mission and core values. Sometimes these theories can be framed in terms of organizational activities that produce immediate organizational outputs, which in turn catalyze outcomes reflected in changing behaviors of clients or partners. Those outcomes contribute to producing longer-term social impacts. In complex environments where results are shaped by many different forces, unambiguous causal links in change theories are very difficult to establish. For most CSOs, however, some theory of change underlies their actions even when conclusive evidence of impact is difficult to find.

Mapping and Prioritizing Organizational Stakeholders

Identifying stakeholders who affect or are affected by CSO strategies is critical to constructing legitimacy and accountability systems that support those strategies. Stakeholder maps can be constructed by asking questions; for example, who is affected by the activity of this CSO? Who asks (or should ask) for information about CSO performance?

Answers to such questions can be used to map key stakeholders and their links to strategic issues. Figure 5.1 maps some of the stakeholders of the Oxfam International "Make Trade Fair" campaign in an international cotton market whose prices are distorted by industrialized countries' subsidies to their own cotton farmers. Stakeholders for the value creation

Figure 5.1 Oxfam Stakeholders in the Cotton Campaign

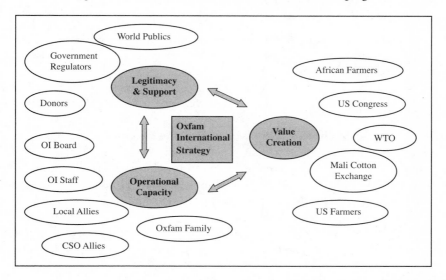

issue include African cotton farmers, the Malian cotton-marketing agency that buys their cotton, advocacy targets such as the World Trade Organization (WTO) and the US Congress, and US cotton farmers. The stakeholders for the legitimacy and support issue include the donors who support Oxfam, government regulators that oversee its work, and the US publics whose perceptions of Oxfam's legitimacy affect its influence with US policymakers. Operational capacity stakeholders include staff at Oxfam International, its board, Oxfam family members, and their local and transnational allies in the global campaign.

Note that stakeholders may appear in different places on this map. Governments can confer legitimacy and support, but they may also be targets of advocacy campaigns. Boards may be part of both operational capacity and the legitimacy and support environment. Determining where key actors fit in stakeholder maps often requires close assessment of how the actors relate to the CSO's strategy and theory of change.

Prioritizing stakeholders involves assessing how much the CSO should pay attention to their accountability claims. The CSO should ask three questions about each stakeholder: [5]

- Are we accountable on *legal* grounds to this stakeholder? Are we answerable in terms of laws, regulations, formal policies, or "customs having the force of law"?

- Are we accountable on *normative* grounds to this stakeholder? Are we answerable in terms of core values and norms of the society, the domain, or our own organization?

- Are we accountable on *pragmatic* grounds to this stakeholder? Are we answerable because the stakeholder can impose high practical costs for failures to respond?

Stakeholder maps often reveal large discrepancies in CSO attention to different stakeholders. Many CSOs that have not devoted explicit attention to strategic choices about accountabilities become accountable primarily to stakeholders that can impose high costs in pragmatic terms, such as donors or government regulators who can stop funding or enforce regulations. "Upward" and "outward" accountabilities to powerful external stakeholders are often better developed than "downward" and "inward" accountabilities to clients or staff. For many CSOs, however, strong moral commitments press for paying attention to less powerful stakeholders, such as disaster victims or marginalized groups. Creating accountability to stakeholders with less voice often requires actively constructing systems that enable their input.

Assessing Legitimacy and Accountability Demands

Legitimacy and accountability are different concepts and pose somewhat different demands and challenges. Legitimacy reflects a widely shared sense among publics and stakeholders in the context that the agency's existence and activities are appropriate and justified. Accountability involves more specific relationships in which immediate stakeholders have some claim on the agency's performance. A CSO might have legitimacy with the wider community of donor agencies but be accountable to the donors that have made contributions to its work. It might seek legitimacy with the public in general but be accountable to members of the public it claims to serve directly. A CSO might seek legitimacy with the agencies whose policies it seeks to influence, but perceive itself to be accountable to members or beneficiaries of that campaign.

Assessing legitimacy demands often starts with responding to challenges to the CSO's activity. Demands for legitimacy are often framed in terms of "illegitimate behavior." The US Trade Representative questioned the legitimacy of Oxfam International's work with Southern governments at the WTO meetings in Cancun after those governments decided to reject what they believed was an unfair deal from the Northern governments. In other cases, work on legitimacy emerges from preparing for an anticipated challenge. CSOs may recognize the potential for problems before they happen and systematically assess their own bases and resources for legitimacy. When Oxfam International began to work on transnational policy campaigns as part of its overall strategy, it recognized that those campaigns would require building new bases of legitimacy with a wide range of stakeholders.

Assessing legitimacy involves articulating the kinds of legitimacy required by the CSO's strategy and change theory, the bases on which that legitimacy can rest, and the gaps between existing and needed legitimacy. One approach to legitimacy assessment is to articulate the CSO's perception of the bases for its legitimacy as a prelude to examining discrepancies between its assessment and that of key stakeholders. Legitimacy expectations can be assessed in terms of the six sources of legitimacy identified in Chapter 3: [6]

- *Regulatory legitimacy* is grounded in compliance with legal requirements.

- *Associational legitimacy* comes from association with others seen to be legitimate.

- *Performance legitimacy* is based on expertise, capacities, and resources that meet the interests of stakeholders.

- *Political legitimacy* is rooted in representing an important constituency.

- *Normative legitimacy* comes from embodying and acting for widely held values and norms.

- *Cognitive legitimacy* comes from behavior that fits widely held conceptual categories about good practice.

Many of the most discrepant assessments of CSO legitimacy emerge in the course of advocacy campaigns, as targets question the legitimacy of CSOs to criticize or advocate on the issues. Oxfam International, for example, perceived that its legitimacy for influencing governments in the Cancun WTO meetings came from performance legitimacy (grounded in its knowledge about trade policy) and normative legitimacy (from its support for fair trade). The targets of the campaign, such as the US Trade Representative, claimed that Oxfam was not elected to represent anyone and therefore had no political legitimacy to advise governments.

Since the "Group of 21" developing-country governments made substantial use of Oxfam's advice, it appears that they accepted its claim to performance and/or normative legitimacy. If Oxfam had been equally successful with the governments of the industrialized countries, the meetings might have produced breakthroughs on trade issues instead of a deadlock. In the months following the Cancun meetings, the US Trade

Representative and Oxfam engaged in public sparring about Oxfam's role; both parties sought to influence the ongoing discourse over the future roles of CSOs and the importance of "leveling the playing field" for future negotiations.

Was Oxfam International in fact an "unaccountable loose cannon" at the Cancun meetings? The critics were correct in arguing that Oxfam was not elected to represent affected groups, who were already represented by national government delegates. On the other hand, Oxfam provided policy advice to developing-country governments who needed experience and expertise to assess the issues. Legitimacy from performance and normative bases can be buttressed by accountability to technical standards or principled adherence to values and norms.

Since many criticisms of CSOs are couched in terms of accountability, *assessing accountability claims* can be a powerful tool for responding to legitimacy challenges. Assessing accountabilities involves exploring current expectations and performance in key stakeholder relationships. This may require assessing the substantive expectations, underlying models, and accountability priorities that underpin the relationship between CSO and stakeholder. Like legitimacy demands, accountability demands may emerge as explicit challenges by existing stakeholders or as potential challenges based on an analysis of the CSO's strategy and its impact on different stakeholders.

CSOs may feel answerable to stakeholders on one or more dimensions. Oxfam International, for example, feels accountable to partner associations of cotton farmers on normative grounds, though those associations have relatively little legal or pragmatic base on which to compel compliance with their requests. Oxfam has both normative and pragmatic reasons for being accountable to its allies in policy campaigns, since those campaigns depend on mobilizing many different actors and resources for long-term success. Setting priorities among stakeholders may be particularly important when the costs of responding to their demands are high or when their demands are in conflict—a situation that is quite common in transnational advocacy.

There is no easy formula for weighting normative, legal, and pragmatic considerations to decide which stakeholders have highest priority. For many CSOs, assessing accountabilities produces a discomfiting awareness that their existing systems tend to emphasize legal and pragmatic terms, with the result that powerful stakeholders get more attention than stakeholders who rank high in terms of CSO values and missions. In theory CSO leaders might want an exhaustive analysis of accountabilities to all stakeholders, but in practice the sheer variety of stakeholders compels focusing on the most important. Oxfam International works in dozens of countries on a wide range of advocacy, development, and disaster relief projects. CSOs that assign high priority to accounting to all their myriad stakeholders may succumb to a multiple-stakeholder induced paralysis rather than focusing on accomplishing their strategies and missions. But if they avoid grappling with the issue, they are likely to prioritize powerful stakeholders at the expense of less powerful ones—thus ignoring constituencies central to their missions.

Assessments of legitimacy and accountability demands often evolve over time as CSOs grapple with emerging challenges and dynamics. It is useful, however, to begin early to examine how the CSO and its key stakeholders frame their legitimacy and accountability relations—particularly if there are significant discrepancies in how the parties understand the issues.

Articulating Aspirations for the Future

The assessment process culminates in articulating aspirations for a future in which the CSO's legitimacy and accountability enable it to carry out its strategy and accomplish its mission. Much of the challenge CSOs face in grappling with legitimacy and accountability questions grows out of their association with responsibility and punishment for failure. As one analyst has put it, "Everyone wants to hold others accountable, but no one wants to be held accountable."[7] It is clear that efforts to become more legitimate and more accountable can be costly in energy, time, and resources—who would want to invest in such efforts if they largely serve to make civil society leaders more vulnerable to challenge or criticism?

So exploring the value of enhanced legitimacy and accountability is important for building support for that investment. Thus for Oxfam International, the Cancun negotiations and the Doha Round of trade negotiations were seen as a limited success in that the rich countries did not impose more unfair trade regimes on an aroused developing-country coalition. On the other hand, the goal of creating a fairer global trade regime for the developing countries was not achieved. So for Oxfam, a desired future state might include a coalition that has sufficient legitimacy with both Northern and Southern negotiators to construct new and equitable trade rules, not just block the imposition of unfair institutions.

The creation of aspirations for future legitimacy and accountability potentially mobilizes energy and commitment for going forward. Experience suggests that major changes in legitimacy and accountability systems often emerge from externally induced crises, so it may be difficult to engage in systematic initiatives without crises to underline their urgency. At the same time, supplementing crisis motivations with positive visions of the future can be a key element in constructive change processes—so attention to articulating compelling aspirations for legitimacy and accountability can be vital.

Enhancing Organizational Legitimacy

Enhancing organizational legitimacy is difficult, since legitimacy tends to be established or eroded over long periods and depends on distant and amorphous audiences such as "the public" or "the donor community" or "international financial institutions." In national contexts it is sometimes possible to be certified by national authorities and so quite quickly attain wider credibility, but widely recognized authorities and authorization are less common in the transnational arena. So enhancing legitimacy may be a long-term process involving many different actors.

The assessment process clarifies the identity and goals of the CSO, its important stakeholders, and the kinds of legitimacy demands that have been posed either by direct challenges to its legitimacy or by organizational and contextual changes that undermine prior bases for legitimacy. A CSO with aspirations for the future can use those elements to focus attention on how enhanced legitimacy will help the organization achieve. its mission or expand its impacts.

Chapter 4 discussed several strategies for enhancing organizational legitimacy. The first three approaches—conforming to legitimacy expectations, informing stakeholders about that compliance, and associating with legitimate symbols and people—all involve articulating the bases of legitimacy vital to the agency and then mobilizing resources and activities to show that the organization's existence and activity are justified by those bases. The fourth approach involves constructing arguments and integrating them into existing discourses in ways that construct new legitimacy standards and expectations for the CSO.

Utilizing Existing Legitimacy Expectations

One approach to dealing with challenges to organizational legitimacy is to ensure that the CSO *conforms to existing legitimacy standards and expectations.* This approach provides the basis for responding that legitimacy challenges are incorrect or misinformed. Ensuring that the organization does in fact comply with key standards can forestall challenges or resolve them quickly. An agency charged with financial improprieties might respond by offering audited accounts that meet legal standards. Oxfam International, accused of being unelected and unrepresentative of any constituency with a stake in the Cancun discussions, might demonstrate that it had been appointed to represent a regional association of West African cotton growers. This management strategy assumes that the characteristics of legitimate actors are understood and agreed upon, and that compliance with the resulting standards is feasible for the CSO.

A second strategy is to articulate the relevant bases for legitimacy and *inform key stakeholders why the agency is legitimate* in those terms. In some circumstances, for example, stakeholders criticize CSO legitimacy on the basis of the wrong standards. Educating stakeholders about legitimacy bases may be more important than proving that the CSO meets those standards. Oxfam International does not see its legitimacy in the Cancun discussions as being grounded in political representation of cotton formers, but rather on normative and performance bases. It expects to be seen as a credible source of important information and to appeal to public support for widely held values and norms for fairness. So Oxfam's response to the criticism that it is unelected might be "Yes . . . but that is not the basis on which we claim to be heard in this matter." Whether Oxfam offers good policy analyses is still up for criticism, but that criticism would draw on the standards of research or policy analysis or ethics rather than on the political representation of some stakeholder group.

A third legitimacy management strategy is to *associate with institutions, practices, and people that are widely seen to be legitimate.* Adopting organizational elements common in highly regarded agencies, recruiting board members who have credibility and legitimacy as eminent persons, and building alliances with other well-respected agencies are all ways to enhance legitimacy by association. Oxfam International, for example, is composed of national organizations that have often recruited highly regarded board members whose reputations shine reflected glory on the organization. Perhaps more important, Oxfam has built alliances with a wide range of highly regarded civil society organizations. For some of its members, choices to dissociate themselves from some stakeholders have also had powerful implications for enhancing their legitimacy with others. For example, the fact that Oxfam America accepts no funds from the US government has enhanced its reputation as an independent voice that can "speak truth to power."

Organizations can make use of several strategies at the same time, as is implied in the preceding discussion. These approaches make use of existing expectations and understanding about civil society legitimacy. But in some circumstances, existing standards of legitimacy are themselves a problem, so constructing new legitimacy standards is necessary.

Constructing New Legitimacy Standards and Expectations

The fourth approach to responding to legitimacy challenges is to *construct new standards* that enable the organization to carry out innovative programs that might otherwise be seen as illegitimate. The standards involved in the first three approaches may be either rule-based sources of legitimacy or negotiated standards that emerge from debate and discourse among many stakeholders. Constructing new standards in the transnational arena almost always involves negotiations among many interested parties that produce results that are not necessarily predictable from prior experience.

New standards and bases for legitimacy may have to be constructed to deal with changing strategies and contexts. Oxfam International's national members recognized in the mid-1990s both the hazards of globalization—such as the possibility that mismanagement of one national Oxfam could harm the reputation and identity of the whole family—and the opportunities posed by an increasingly interdependent world—such as influencing global policies that affect poor and marginalized populations everywhere. The development of Oxfam International has involved building analytic frameworks to underpin the "Make Trade Fair" campaign; debates within and among the Oxfams as well as with other international NGOs concerned with trade; reorganizing for transnational strategy development and program management; and an ongoing series of negotiations with allies, publics, and advocacy targets who apply irrelevant or distorting standards to assess the legitimacy of emerging initiatives.

New standards and legitimacy bases may also be required when existing expectations do not permit needed innovations and activities. In some cases the creation of CSOs and the implementation of their strategies have involved frontal attacks on existing expectations and norms. Transparency International, for example, directly challenged the prevailing view that corruption was "part of the way things are" that could not be altered, even though its corrosive impacts on development projects was widely recognized. Transparency's support for national reform movements has catalyzed a wide range of national initiatives, and its work on transnational initiatives, such as the Extractive Industries Transparency Initiative, has in many ways revolutionized expectations about corruption. Although corruption persists, the assumption that it is inevitable has been significantly eroded. Meanwhile, Transparency is busy constructing new standards and expectations about legitimate practice on several fronts.

Constructing Organizational Accountability Systems

Strategic choices to align stakeholder accountabilities with mission and strategy call for systems to support and implement that alignment. *Accountability systems* are organizational arrangements for recognizing, negotiating, and responding to obligations to stakeholders. They may be formally defined in explicit expectations about how the CSO will account to stakeholders or informally recognized and understood. Accountability systems may include tools (such as disclosures, reports, and performance evaluations), processes (such as participation or self-regulation), and combinations of tools and processes (such as social auditing).[8] They provide vehicles for stakeholder participation in setting expectations, ensuring transparency, evaluating performance, and enabling complaints and redress if expectations are not met.[9] Building accountability systems begins with assessing accountabilities. Four other tasks are required to construct effective accountability systems: (1) negotiating expectations with key stakeholders, (2) creating performance measurement systems, (3) enabling consequences for performance that succeeds or fails to meet expected levels, and (4) building organization capacities to implement the system over the longer term.

Negotiating Stakeholder Expectations

Many CSOs pay little attention to discussing accountability expectations unless powerful stakeholders demand information. But negotiating expectations across stakeholders has several advantages. CSOs that face competing accountability claims can reduce misunderstanding and conflict by setting realistic expectations. Involving stakeholders in defining indicators of performance can shape their participation in joint work, which is particularly important when results are co-produced. Negotiating expectations clarifies the variety of claims on the CSO—even when those expectations are vague and conflicting—and reduces unrealistic hopes that the CSO can respond fully to all its stakeholders.

Stakeholders vary in their abilities to negotiate accountability expectations: donor agencies may have clear standards and considerable capacity to impose them, while clients are often less able to protect their interests. It is not surprising that many CSO activities are perceived as "donor-driven," since donors are often the major voices heard in negotiating accountability expectations. Paying explicit attention to a range of stakeholders can reduce donor dominance of accountability systems by default. Oxfam International has recognized that accountability to less powerful constituencies is a critical issue. Some of its members have invested substantial resources in negotiating expectations for program implementation and accountability with local partners, and their organizational cultures emphasize mutual influence among partners rather than command-and-control decision making.

Negotiating accountabilities with all stakeholders can be a daunting task. Negotiations should begin with high-priority stakeholders, particularly those whose voices have been less often heard in the past. Negotiating with less powerful stakeholders may require special efforts to organize them for participation and shared decision making. Not all negotiations end in agreements, of course, but even articulating areas of disagreement can be the grounds for joint learning and mutual accountability in the future.

The challenge of negotiating accountabilities becomes especially acute when CSOs are in the midst of strategic changes. When Oxfam International added global policy campaigns to its emphases on disaster relief and local capacity building, the reverberations were felt throughout the agency. Under the new strategy, strategic priorities increasingly emerged from discussions at the international level rather than from national and regional concerns. Support for new local projects and extension of old projects increasingly became linked to their relevance to global campaigns, so old expectations for influence and accountability had to be renegotiated.

The nature of the negotiations will also turn on assumptions about the underlying model of accountability relations. In principal-agent accountability, negotiations focus on the interests of the principal and agreements that protect those interests. In mutual accountability negotiations, the parties articulate shared values and commitments and build common understanding about their responsibilities in achieving joint goals. The emphasis in principal-agent agreements is on setting the right incentives for agents; the emphasis in mutual accountability is on building trust in each other to invest seriously in achieving shared visions. The emphasis at Oxfam has been on building partnerships and mutual accountability for local action. As strategic decisions moved toward policy-advocacy campaigns, staff and partners came under pressure to extend mutual accountability relations across international boundaries and multiple levels, and the negotiation of shared expectations became significantly more difficult.

Creating Performance Measurement Systems

Negotiating expectations for accountability involves decisions about how CSO performance can be measured. That performance is often difficult to assess: results such as improved services, enhanced capacities, or policy reforms can be difficult to measure, distant in time, and subject to a variety of other influences. Because of these challenges, performance measures for CSOs are often inherently ambiguous. Different stakeholders may want different forms of assessment, so CSOs have to make judgments about what measures are most appropriate. At least three quite different forms of assessment may be useful to CSOs, depending on the stakeholders to whom they seek to be accountable: (1) *impact assessment* that focuses on long-term results, (2) *story construction* that frames CSO activity in a value and historical context, and (3) *institutional analysis* that regards the agency as a sustainable social phenomenon.

Impact assessment focuses on assessing how well the organization produces the outputs, outcomes, and impacts indicated by its value creation

Figure 5.2 Performance Measurement and Social Impacts

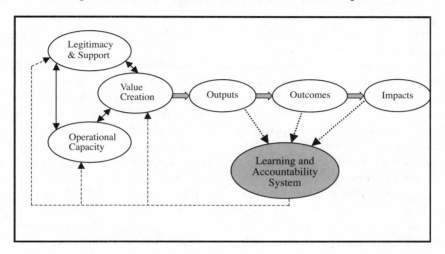

or change theory.[10] Figure 5.2 combines the strategic triangle with the chain of outputs, outcomes, and impacts predicted by its theory of value creation. The dotted arrows suggest areas from which performance indicators might be drawn, including immediate organizational outputs, outcomes in terms of changed client behaviors, and longer term social impacts. For Oxfam's policy campaigns, outputs might include press releases printed and coalitions supported, outcomes might be journalists writing sympathetic stories and coalitions lobbying legislatures, and impacts might be new policies implemented and enhanced credibility with policymakers. Dashed arrows from the learning and accountability system suggest how measures might be used to clarify or redefine the value to be created, demonstrate that value to authorizers and supporters, and enable learning that improves operational capacity.

While many analysts have argued for focusing on the outcomes and impacts at the right side of Figure 5.2, those results are often sufficiently distant in time and space from CSO activity to be less useful for managing performance than more immediate indicators such as outputs. Studies of long-term impacts can strengthen the theoretical links along the value chain to make outputs and immediate outcomes useful proxies for long-term impacts. Thus impact studies have indicated that Oxfam-supported policy analyses and coalition building with Mozambican women (outputs) contributed to the legislature revising laws to enable women to own property (outcomes) that will greatly improve the lives of widows and their children (impact). This impact analysis has reinforced the theory that organizing coalitions and providing policy analysis support can be important elements of a change theory for enhancing women's voices in many issues.

Story construction focuses on framing the values of the CSO, articulating its history, and providing a meaningful context within which to understand its present activities.[11] While impact analysis assesses key components of a change theory for stakeholders interested in impacts, story construction focuses on providing a meaningful framework that can guide and motivate action by staff and allies, particularly action by poor and marginalized constituents. Such stories draw on local histories and values, often integrating rationales for CSO activities with religious traditions and local perspectives that are central to key stakeholders. They provide bases for stakeholders to explain to themselves and others why they commit time and energy to the initiative, and they can be powerful incentives for ongoing action in difficult circumstances. Articulating stories that enable diverse stakeholders to justify working together has been central to success in Oxfam's work with communities that engage in extractive industries to reduce environmental consequences or to ensure that some extracted value comes back to the communities.

Institutional analysis recognizes that agencies and expectations can be institutionalized as enduring social phenomena even when their explicit contributions to positive impacts or to social meaning are not clearly established. Agencies can become embedded in a society's expectations and expressions in ways that sustain their support and legitimacy independent of their objective contributions to any group or the society at large.[12] CSOs may become infused with social value so that their termination is not an acceptable result even if they fall on hard times. Oxfam Great Britain, for example, has been a national fixture for five decades, running hundreds of shops that serve people throughout the country. It has become a national institution that is likely to continue to benefit from the support of thousands of private donors as well as grants from government agencies even if its desired impacts are very difficult to demonstrate. Institutional analysis involves examining indicators of how stakeholders regard the CSO and the extent to which it has become legally, normatively, and cognitively part of "the way things are" in its social context. Such institutions persist even without being able to clearly demonstrate that they produce well-defined public goods.

There are, in short, a number of ways that the "performance" of CSOs may be conceived and measured. Evidence of impacts, stories that establish compelling social meanings, and institutionalization of organizational roles and identities are all relevant to assessing CSOs. For CSOs concerned with describing their performance to a wide range of stake-holders, evidence about their value creation outputs, outcomes, and impacts may be particularly valuable, so Figure 5.2 emphasizes that set of concerns. But attention to stories and institutional roles may be very important ways of presenting those data. Performance indicators, data collection methods, and interpretations of results can be tailored to specific CSO strategies, programs, and stakeholders. Negotiating expectations can engage stakeholders in identifying relevant indicators. Constructing a learning and accountability system that produces relevant and credible indicators for high-priority stakeholders is central to enhancing CSO accountability.

Enabling Performance Consequences

Accountability systems require organizational arrangements to communicate results and to enable consequences for success and failure in meeting expectations. How can different stakeholders learn about CSO performance indicators, and what capacities do they have to hold CSOs accountable for good and bad performance?

Communications systems provide stakeholders with information about CSO performance, from reports and evaluations of specific programs to annual reports and audits of the CSO as a whole. Existing systems for communicating performance results are often closely tied to stakeholders who can demand performance data. When CSOs become widely visible as consumers of public or voluntary resources, media attention may make information about their performance more widely available. Oxfam International, for example, is often the subject of critical media attention. So some kinds of information, such as scandals about use of funds or controversial positions taken by some Oxfam family members, are quickly communicated around the world. On the other hand, like many other CSOs, Oxfam is less able to communicate information about its work to grassroots partners who do not speak English. It has become a high priority for Oxfam International to develop systems for enabling wider participation and engagement in local project assessment.

Rewards and sanctions for CSO performance are more available to some stakeholders than to others. Marginalized villagers in developing countries, for example, cannot easily challenge CSOs, and staff may find it difficult to question the performance of their superiors. But CSOs can create systems for sharing information about and learning from organizational activities with a wide range of stakeholders, from conferences with staff and allies to reflect on program delivery to workshops with clients to assess program performance and improvement. ActionAid has developed an Accountability, Learning and Planning System (Alps) that emphasizes involvement of clients in designing, assessing, and learning from program experience. CSOs that use value-based appeals for support are particularly vulnerable to charges that they do not live up to those values. CSOs who have "named and shamed" business, government, and intergovernmental actors for deviations from good practice can be seriously embarrassed by revelations that they do not meet the standards they demand of others. Transparency International, for example, was embarrassed by national branches that engaged in corrupt practices.[13] When targets of policy influence campaigns can show that CSOs do not in fact speak for grassroots groups they claim to represent, the credibility of the CSOs can be impaired with larger publics as well.[14]

The risk of performance sanctions and the possibility of performance incentives can help CSOs resist temptation to cover up problems. Some CSOs have concluded that the consequences of cover-ups are sometimes worse than those of open discussion of problems. When Oxfam recognized that staff in Indonesia had pilfered funds designated for post-tsunami relief, it disclosed the problem to the media (with some trepidation) even before its managers had fully assessed it. To the agency's surprise, the resulting worldwide publicity commented favorably on their frankness about the issue. When CSOs opt for participatory approaches and accountability to local clients, they may balance client demands against donor pressures for control and accountability and so preserve flexibility to respond to local needs and conditions. Creating systems that strengthen accountability pressures from otherwise unheard clients and allies may offset stakeholder pressures that would otherwise divert programs from local needs and concerns. After all, donors and regulators often agree with CSOs that enhancing the capacities and voices of grassroots populations is central to long-term sustainable development.

Developing Organizational Support Systems

Operating organizational accountability systems requires resources and ongoing investments by staff and CSO leaders. Sustainable accountability systems require expertise and capacities in the organization and commitment from CSO leaders to pay attention to the information they produce. To the extent that accountability is seen as an externally imposed demand with little connection to CSO missions and strategies, the investment in organizational support systems is likely to be relatively minimal and subject to diversion. If accountability is seen as a vital element of strategy implementation and mission accomplishment, leaders are more likely to invest in ongoing organizational support for accountability systems.

The growing concern in the transnational arena about legitimacy and accountability has encouraged many leaders of transnational CSOs to invest more resources in accountability systems and the organizational resources and expertise required to support them. Oxfam International and several of its members have explicitly committed to enhancing their capacity for learning and accountability in their emerging strategic plans. Oxfam America, for example, has created a Learning, Evaluation and Accountability Program that is building state-of-the-art systems for assessing its programs and learning from its experience. Both Oxfam International and Oxfam America have recognized the critical importance of ongoing learning as well as accountability for their future effectiveness.

Using Organizational Accountability Systems

Accountability systems that generate information about performance provide CSOs with a number of opportunities for strengthening the agency and its impacts. Those opportunities include (1) strengthening legitimacy and support, (2) building operational capacity, (3) organizational learning that enhances value creation, and (4) enabling interorganizational discourses that can shape the larger domains in which the CSO participates.

Strengthening Legitimacy and Support

Building and using accountability systems provides a base for responding to legitimacy questions. As CSOs have become more visible and influential with governments, multinational corporations, intergovernmental organizations, and other large-scale actors, they are increasingly asked, "Whom do you represent?" or "To whom are you accountable?" The implication is that "unelected NGOs" do not have a legitimate voice in many transnational and intersectoral discussions.

CSO leaders can develop initial answers to such questions from assessing the CSO's bases for legitimacy and articulating its primary accountabilities in terms of its mission and strategy. Accountability systems provide information about "to whom" and "for what" the CSO is accountable. They also offer systematic data on CSO performance, arrangements for communicating those results, and mechanisms that enable stakeholders to hold the agency accountable. When Oxfam America assembles a multiyear review of programs in several countries that campaign to improve women's rights or press mining companies to promote local development, that review can be used to build the organization's political, performance, associational, and normative legitimacy. Those results can also be used to solicit long-term support and resources from a wide range of local, national, and international stakeholders.

Information generated by accountability systems is useful for explaining CSO work to many interested parties. But the existence of the system is in itself an answer to questions about accountabilities and how they are met. Organizational accountability systems clarify why CSO strategies are appropriate for accomplishing their missions, who key stakeholders are, how they are given information about agency activity, and how they exercise influence to hold the agency accountable. So the leadership thinking that creates accountability systems can support claims to organizational and institutional legitimacy.

Building Operational Capacity

Organizational accountability systems can also be used to enhance CSO operational capacities. The analysis of organizational strategies and change theories that connect activities to missions and impacts can foster redefinitions of organizational architectures and individual roles for implementing those strategies.

Organizational architectures define the tasks, formal structures and systems, informal arrangements, and human resources required to implement strategies and social change theories.[15] When Oxfam added global policy advocacy to its relief and local development activities, the strategy change required architectural changes at both national and international levels to create new capacity. Coordination of global activities required that Oxfam International build capacity to keep family members from duplicating or undermining each other's contributions, and family members were soon called to surrender some autonomy and authority for international strategic direction and program implementation. Family members soon learned that transnational advocacy campaigns required coordinated communications, media relations, and advocacy with both Northern and Southern governments. That coordination required task forces across local and regional programs, enhanced communications and constituency building, and expanded policy analysis and advocacy capacity. The change also shifted responsibility for many strategic decisions from country staff of member organizations to Oxfam International, a shift that understandably generated considerable resistance.

The analyses required to develop an organizational accountability system can also be used to define individual roles and responsibilities. Clarifying strategic directions and assessing how programs fit into change theories can also help define expectations for staff members in a system that sets goals and reward systems to enhance performance of key activities. Performance measures for particular roles or departments focus attention and resources on accomplishing critical tasks: CSO leaders can assess, reward, and promote staff on the basis of how well they meet those challenges. As CSOs find themselves under pressure to do more with less, their ability to create systems that support high performance will become increasingly critical.

Enhancing Value Creation

Organizational accountability systems can also contribute to organizational learning on the creation of value and other strategic issues. *Learning at the operational level* is essential for CSOs that operate in volatile contexts and seek to foster constructive social change. Information from learning and accountability systems can be used for program learning that enhances performance of core activities. In delivering disaster relief and rehabilitation programs, for example, Oxfam International has learned that it is more effective to name a country lead agency that has developed long-term linkages to local partners and can coordinate resources from other family members than it is to have multiple members working independently in the same region. The value of increased coordination became clear as Oxfam International assessed the costs and gains of multiple programs operating independently of one another. As this example illustrates, data from accountability systems can be used for operational learning that enhances immediate value creation.

Organizational learning may also take place at the *strategic level,* where decisions about evolving responses to contextual changes are made. Oxfam International, as a transnational coordinator, is itself a product of strategic learning by the Oxfam family. Assessing the family's long-term impacts on world poverty and the risks to the family's identity from lack of member coordination led to the creation of Oxfam International and its growing integration of its members into a close-knit family. Investing in organizational learning made possible by accountability systems can test and validate (or invalidate) the change theories that shape CSO strategy and activities. The results can be disconfirming and discomfiting. But there are few substitutes for a capacity to learn when agencies operate in complex and rapidly changing environments in which both organizational and social learning are at a premium.[16]

Catalyzing Domain Discourse

As more CSOs grapple with the implications of legitimacy and accountability to multiple stakeholders, they also identify issues that affect other domain actors as well. As the Oxfams have sought to influence global policies as well as to provide relief and catalyze local development, they have identified issues—such as relations with the UN, relations with corporations, problems of climate change, and legitimacy and accountability issues—that merit debate and discussion with other CSOs. When one CSO grapples with defining legitimacy bases or constructing accountability systems, other actors in the domains in which they operate may be stimulated to grapple with similar questions. The press for domain debates and discourses on the issues is expanded if problems of one member can affect many others. The future of Oxfam International as an effective transnational advocate may be greatly influenced by the behavior of other CSOs that have invested less energy and fewer resources in accountability. The current relatively favorable public perceptions of CSOs could be greatly affected by a few highly visible abuses—and it is clear that many global actors would be happy to publicize such abuses. The growing interest in legitimacy and accountability issues among key CSOs can be expected to catalyze more debates and discourses in many domains in which CSOs operate—a topic to be discussed in more detail in Chapter 6.

Summary

The growing influence and visibility of transnational civil society organizations has produced increasing concern with their legitimacy and accountability. But the diversity of CSO stakeholders and the lack of international societal ideals or negotiated domain standards can make easy response to those concerns difficult. CSOs can make strategic choices that prioritize stakeholders, articulate and enhance legitimacy bases, and define and align accountability systems with their missions and strategies.

Assessing legitimacy and accountabilities involves defining the CSO; articulating its mission, goals, and strategy; mapping and prioritizing its stakeholders; assessing legitimacy and accountability demands; and defining aspirations for a desired future. Enhancing legitimacy may involve clarifying how the CSO meets present standards of legitimacy or constructing new standards that allow for innovative activity or solving emerging problems. Constructing accountability systems involves negotiating expectations with stakeholders, creating performance measurement systems, enabling performance consequences, and creating organization resources to support learning and accountability. Using accountability systems can strengthen CSO legitimacy and support, build operational capacity, enhance value creation in operational and strategic terms, and catalyze domain discourses about field-wide issues. The challenges to CSO leaders of grappling with credibility issues are substantial. So are the potential rewards.

Even more challenging (and perhaps even more rewarding) are the issues involved in the credibility of multiorganization domains. The next three chapters focus on those challenges in three kinds of domains.

Notes

1. See Bolman, L. G. and Deal, T. E., *Reframing Organizations: Artistry, Choice and Leadership* (San Francisco: Jossey-Bass, 2003); Morgan, G., *Images of Organization* (Newbury Park, CA: Sage, 1986).

2. Mintzberg, H., and McHugh, A., "Strategy Formation in an Adhocracy," *Administrative Science Quarterly*, 30 (1985): 160–197; Smillie, I. and Hailey, J., *Managing for Change: Leadership, Strategy and Management in Asian NGOs* (London: Earthscan, 2001). For an analysis of the importance of loosely organized networks in knowledge-based societies, see Adler, P. S., "Market, Hierarchy and Trust: The Knowledge Economy and the Future of Capitalism," *Organization Science*, 12, no. 2 (2001): 215–234.

3. Moore, M., "Managing for Value: Organizational Strategy in For-profit, Nonprofit, and Governmental Organizations," *Nonprofit and Voluntary Sector Quarterly*, 29, no. 1, Supplement (2000): 183–204; and Moore, M. H., *Creating Public Value: Strategic Management in Government* (Cambridge, MA: Harvard University Press, 1995).

4. Brown, L. David, and Moore, Mark H., "Accountability, Strategy and International Nongovernmental Organizations," *Nonprofit and Voluntary Sector Quarterly*, 30, no. 3 (2001): 569–587.

5. See Brown and Moore, "Accountability, Strategy and International Nongovernmental Organizations," (2001). See also Brown, L. David, Cohen, David, Edwards, Michael, Eigen, Peter, Heinrich, Finn, Martin, Nigel, Moore, Mark, Murillo, Gabriel, Naidoo, Kumi, Pongsapich, Amara and Scholte, Jan Aart, "Civil Society Legitimacy: A Discussion Guide" in *Practice-Research Engagement and Civil Society in a Globalizing World*, ed. L. David Brown (Washington, DC: CIVICUS: World Alliance for Citizen Participation, 2001): 31–48.

6. This framework is based on those articulated by Jacobs, Alex, Jepson, Paul and Nicholls, Alex, *Improving the Performance of Social Purpose Organizations: The Strategic Management of Organizational Legitimacy.* (Cambridge, UK: Skoll Center for Social Entrepreneurship, 2006), especially pp 9–15; Brown et al, "Civil Society Legitimacy: A Discussion Guide" (2001): 31–48; and Suchman, M. C., "Managing Legitimacy: Strategic and Institutional Approaches," *Academy of Management Review*, 20, no. 3 (1995): 517–610.

7. Behn, Robert, "Rethinking Accountability in Education: How Should Who Hold Whom Accountable for What?" *International Public Management Journal*, 6, no. 1 (2003): 43–73.

8. Ebrahim, A., "Accountability in Practice: Mechanisms for NGOs," *World Development*, 31, no. 3 (2003): 813–829.

9. Blagescu, M., "What Makes Global Organisations Accountable? Reassessing the Global Accountability Framework," Working Paper 101, One World Trust, 2004.

10. See materials on the Keystone website at http://www. keystonereporting.org/. For a manual on constructing sequences of outputs, outcomes and impacts, see the W. K. Kellogg Foundation website at http://www.wkkf.org/Pubs/Tools/Evaluation/Pub3669.pdf.

11. See Ganz, Marshall, "The Power of Story in Social Movements," prepared for the annual meeting of the American Sociological Association, 2001.

12. DiMaggio, P. J. and Powell, W. W., "Introduction," in *The New Institutionalism in Organizational Analysis*, ed. W. W. Powell and P. J. DiMaggio (Chicago: University of Chicago Press, 1991): 1–38; Scott, W. R., *Institutions and Organizations* (Thousand Oaks, CA: Sage, 1995).

13. Galtung, F., "A Global Network to Curb Corruption: The Experience of Transparency International," in *The Third Force*, ed. Ann Florini (Tokyo: Japan Center for International Exchange and Washington: Carnegie Endowment for International Peace, 2001): 17–47.

14. Jordan, L. and v. Tuijl, P., "Political Responsibility in Transnational NGO Advocacy," *World Development*, 28, no.12 (2000): 2051–2065.

15. Nadler, D. A., Gerstein, M. S. and Shaw, R. B., eds., *Organizational Architecture: Designs for Changing Organizations* (San Francisco: Jossey-Bass, 1992).

16. See Brown, L. David and Timmer, Vanessa, "Transnational Civil Society and Social Learning," *Voluntas: International Journal of Voluntary and Nonprofit Organizations*, 17, no. 1 (2006): 1–16.

CHAPTER SIX

Negotiating Sector Credibility

How can civil society organizations (CSOs) and their leaders deal with challenges to legitimacy and accountability that threaten harm to the activities and goals of multiorganization domains? The term "domain" refers to multiple organizations with interests in some area of work. Common multiorganization domains include sector associations (in which "sector" refers to an area of civil society activity), advocacy campaigns (which may include actors from different levels), and cross-sector partnerships (in which "sector" refers to civil society, business, and government partners concerned with an issue).[1] Advocacy campaigns and cross-sector partnerships will be discussed in Chapters 7 and 8.

This chapter deals with *sector associations* composed of civil society organizations that have similar missions, strategies, and goals. Examples of civil society sectors include child sponsorship agencies, human rights organizations, microcredit NGOs, and emergency relief organizations. Sector associations become important as CSOs with similar missions and strategies discover that they are interdependent in ways that call for joint action. When Save the Children and Foster Parents Plan began their child sponsorship programs, there were few obvious reasons for them to associate. But the rise of other child sponsorship organizations and their shared interest in countering media attacks encouraged their leaders to join together to counter credibility challenges. The number of civil society actors working in transnational contexts has escalated sharply since World War II: "Formal transnational NGOs have been accumulating at an unprecedented and increasing rate for fifty years."[2] As the number of organizations and their impacts on transnational problems increase, so do their visibility and potential vulnerability to credibility questions.

Strengthening the legitimacy and accountability of civil society sector associations poses challenges that resemble those of strengthening legitimacy and accountability of individual organizations. Multiorganization sector associations, however, differ from single organizations in several ways. First, sector domains are composed of organizations that share some interests but may not recognize themselves as part of a community, so defining a shared sector identity can be critical to joint action. Second, organizations often see other members of the domain as competitors for resources and reputation rather than as collaborators, so cooperation must be constructed rather than assumed. Third, even when domain members recognize their interdependence, they have to create organizational arrangements that can implement collective action on behalf of the sector. So the challenges of enhancing domain credibility pose issues beyond those raised by credibility challenges to a single organization. Negotiating shared understanding and agreements about standards across organizations that engage in similar activities may require dealing with histories of competition as well as building new systems.

The challenges to credibility have been particularly fierce for CSOs engaged in transnational advocacy. Human rights organizations, environmental organizations, and good governance organizations that publicize abuses and hold powerful actors accountable have often catalyzed fierce counterattacks on their legitimacy and accountability. This chapter illustrates the use of sector negotiations to create standards of legitimacy and accountability by describing the case of an association of international advocacy NGOs and networks (IANGOs) that seek to influence international public policies and actions. This association grew out of a series of annual workshops for IANGO leaders to discuss shared concerns and learn from each others' experiences.[3] The network includes organizations concerned with environmental protection, human rights, humanitarian relief, poverty alleviation, good governance, labor rights, women's rights, and a variety of other issues. Over the course of five years it has constructed an "Accountability Charter" for international NGOs that is intended to set accountability standards for international civil society organizations and networks.

This chapter applies the framework of Chapters 3 and 4 to the challenges of strengthening the credibility of sector associations. This chapter will consider (1) assessing the legitimacy and accountability challenges facing the sector, (2) enhancing sector legitimacy, (3) constructing sector accountability systems, and (4) using legitimacy and accountability resources to enhance the sector's transnational roles.

Assessing Sector Legitimacy and Accountability

Legitimacy and accountability standards can be created by negotiations among organizations when it becomes clear that the sector needs common standards to enable its members to pursue their missions effectively.[4] Articulating standards of accountability for a sector can build on the experience and knowledge of domain members to create standards grounded in deep understanding of sector issues and challenges.

But strengthening sector legitimacy and accountability can be politically and intellectually challenging. Five considerations deserve attention when assessing sector legitimacy and accountability: (1) defining the sector and its members, (2) identifying sectorwide goals and strategic issues, (3) mapping sector stakeholders, (4) assessing sector legitimacy and accountability demands, and (5) articulating aspirations for a better future. The next section examines these considerations and illustrates them from the experience of the IANGO Network.

Defining the Sector and Its Members

Communities of organizations vary considerably in how much they see themselves as interdependent and as members of a common sector. Outside observers may perceive interdependencies and reasons for collective action as a sector that are not obvious to sector members themselves. Members often see each other as competitors, particularly if they draw on the same sources of support or promote alternative solutions to similar problems. In the absence of a crisis that affects the sector as a whole, members may be indifferent or even antagonistic to one another. While there may be advantages in cooperation, such as the possibility of mutual learning from experience, bringing sector members together often requires a common threat to the sector as a whole. The child sponsorship NGOs, for example, had been discussing the possibility of constructing shared standards for years before media criticism threatened their donor base and catalyzed collective action to build a sectorwide accountability system.[5] While the benefits of sector standards can be substantial, mobilizing members to construct them may be difficult.

Identifying a convener who is credible and neutral may be vital to enabling joint action. Sometimes neutral third parties can play this convener role; on other occasions a group that includes trusted representatives of major factions can be a credible convener.[6] In the case of the IANGO Network, for example, the initiatives for developing shared standards emerged from the convergence of several factors. The success of many IANGOs in influencing a variety of international policies and problem-solving initiatives catalyzed a backlash from many sources, including many government and business targets of IANGO campaigns. This backlash included a widely publicized conference funded by right-wing foundations and the establishment of an international "NGO Watch" Web site in 2003.

Coincidentally, the IANGO Network held its first meeting a few weeks later. Chief executives of about 20 IANGOs came together at the invitation of neutral conveners—the CIVICUS World Alliance for Citizen Participation and Harvard University's Hauser Center for Nonprofit Organizations—to explore possibilities for mutual learning and support. They rapidly discovered their common interest in responding to credibility challenges posed by the new NGO Watch and the growing backlash to their influence on many transnational issues. So while the IANGO network had little initial cohesion, the reputations of the conveners, the participants' interest in each other, and the threat of external critics encouraged them to explore shared interests. Participants at the initial meeting, hosted by Transparency International in Berlin, identified many areas of mutual interest and asked the conveners to develop a background paper on the legitimacy and accountability of transnational advocacy organizations for discussion at a future meeting.

Identifying Sector Missions, Goals and Strategies

Defining the sector is a first step, but more is required to build a shared sense of interdependence among sector members. What interests are shared and what interests are independent or in conflict? Do the benefits of building a shared sector identity and missions outweigh its potential costs in lost autonomy? Even when the organizations are similar, as in the case of the US child sponsorship organizations, differences in size, maturity, and commitment to learning from others can make building a domain identity and strategy difficult. The higher the costs of domain membership, the more challenging the task of building shared missions, goals, and strategies.

Creating shared strategy and goals for a sector can be framed in terms of a modified version of the strategic triangle. Figure 6.1 portrays a sector association strategic triangle that is organized around a sheaf of strategies of similar members. The gray triangles representing members have their apexes—representing value creation, legitimacy and support, and operational capability—in similar orientations to indicate similar strategies and goals. While sector members may see themselves as quite different, it is their similarities that are important in constructing sector responses to credibility challenges.

The IANGOs were all nonprofit, nongovernmental organizations or networks, but their missions reflected quite different advocacy concerns and agendas. They shared "progressive" values, but that was not enough to justify much investment in joint action. It was not clear to many participants what they would gain from ongoing meetings, let alone joint action. The workshop identified issues of interest to many IANGO leaders— legitimacy and accountability, relations with the UN and corporations, alliances for WTO meetings—and raised the possibilities of continued dialogue and even collective action. But the first workshop did not produce a sense of shared goals or strategies.

The second workshop catalyzed more agreement on shared concerns. Participating CEOs agreed unanimously on goals for an ongoing workshop: helping members learn about effective transnational advocacy;

Figure 6.1 Sector Domain Strategic Triangle

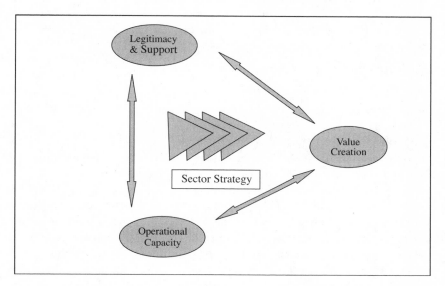

identifying and acting on sector problems, such as legitimacy and accountability; fostering alliance building across organizations and issues; and enabling CEO discussions of leadership challenges. The workshop also constituted a task force of CEOs to draft international NGO standards of accountability for discussion at the next meeting.

Over the next year that task force reviewed codes of conduct from many regions and issues and drafted the International NGO (INGO) Accountability Charter. Participants in the third workshop reviewed the draft Charter and asked the task force to revise it in light of their feedback. During the following year, the IANGOs consulted with their national members about the draft and their concerns about meeting the standards. Many national members raised questions about some standards, such as minimizing environmental footprints, and the legal implications of simultaneously complying with both national codes of conduct and the Charter. At the fourth workshop, twelve of the largest IANGOs became signatories to the revised Charter and held a press conference to announce its creation and plans for its further development and implementation.

The evolution of the Charter reflects an increasing awareness of IANGO interdependence and their shared stake in responding to sector credibility challenges. The Charter was designed to complement existing national codes and articulate core values of the IANGOs, such as commitments to human rights and environmental responsibility, that remained unexpressed in many national standards. Over a five-year period the IANGO leaders increasingly agreed on some shared values, goals, and strategies as a sector association.

Mapping Sector Stakeholders

Agreements on sector goals and strategies can provide the basis for identifying key stakeholders. Some of those stakeholders are *internal* to the sector as members. IANGO leaders agreed that the sector included organizations or networks that spanned many countries to advocate on a wide range of transnational issues. Thus the internal stakeholders included CSOs concerned with poverty alleviation, women's rights, environmental degradation, consumer affairs, indigenous peoples, labor rights, and churches. These internal stakeholders may all be affected by the credibility problems of a single member; for example, the errors in the Greenpeace analysis of the oil remaining in the Brent Spar oil rig have often been used to denigrate the positions of other civil society advocates. Shortcomings of some IANGOs are potentially used to the detriment of the credibility of others.

The identification of *external* stakeholders turns on the nature of the sector and its intended impacts: a sector engaged in emergency or disaster relief will emphasize different stakeholders from a sector concerned with policy advocacy. The nature of sector goals can imply quite different priorities among stakeholders. For example, sectors involved in expensive service delivery put high priorities on legitimacy with and accountability to regulatory agencies and donors; sectors concerned with capacity building emphasize accountability to clients involved in co-producing capacity; and sectors concerned with advocacy are asked about their accountability to members or constituents and their legitimacy with policymaking targets.[7]

Figure 6.2 portrays the IANGO Network and maps some of the internal and external stakeholders considered in the construction of the Accountability Charter. Internal stakeholders include members who have become part of the Network because they have similar orientations toward transnational advocacy, albeit on different issues. The members appear as the sheaf of gray triangles oriented in the same direction at the center of the figure. They are portrayed with relatively similar sizes and shapes to reflect their similar concerns with effective advocacy even though they advocate on a wide range of different issues.

The external stakeholders of the IANGO Network are quite varied. Most members seek to influence target agencies, such as governments, corporations, and the UN, to advance the interests of their primary

Figure 6.2 International Advocacy NGO (IANGO) Sector Stakeholders

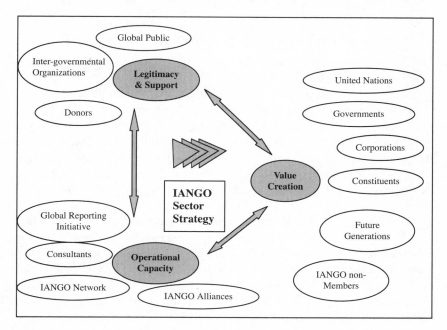

constituents, who are often marginalized and disenfranchised groups. Their value creation activities can affect many other stakeholders, from other IANGOs outside the Network to future generations. Members share a stake in maintaining external stakeholder support and legitimacy for the transnational advocacy sector with donors, intergovernmental organizations, and global publics. The sector can use the operational capacities of willing members, allies, and resource organizations such as the Global Reporting Initiative to create value or to respond to legitimacy and accountability challenges.

It is problematic to prioritize among these stakeholders before the members have generated sector awareness of interdependence and agreement on sectorwide goals and strategies. Sector alliances are likely to attend to "squeaky wheels," such as the vehemently critical participants in the NGO Watch conference and the disgruntled corporate and government advocacy targets who resent public discussion of their shortcomings. Sector alliances may also have to focus special attention on their credibility with their constituents and other low-power stakeholders. Ironically, one ally in keeping alliances accountable to constituents may be advocacy targets, who are often alert to evidence that civil society advocacy does not genuinely represent constituents.

Assessing Sector Legitimacy and Accountability Demands

The legitimacy of the sector turns on the perceptions of a wide range of stakeholders and the general public. Sector accountability refers more specifically to performance expectations by key stakeholders who have direct relationships with the alliance or its members.

Assessing sector legitimacy demands can draw on the bases for legitimacy discussed in Chapter 3—regulatory, associational, performance, political, normative, and cognitive bases for civil society legitimacy. These bases provide a framework for assessing both present challenges to sector legitimacy and potential challenges that might be mounted in the future.

An initial step in assessing legitimacy is to examine the bases on which an agency justifies its existence and activities. Legitimacy bases vary across different activities. Sectors focused on policy advocacy, for example, are often challenged as if their primary legitimacy is based in representation of a constituency: "Who elected you?" For some IANGOs, such as labor federations or networks of indigenous people's organizations, political representation of key constituencies is in fact a critical source of legitimacy. For many others, however, legitimacy in advocacy is not grounded in political representation. Some IANGOs, such as Transparency International, base their legitimacy on performance expertise and information that is of pragmatic value to their targets. Others draw legitimacy from widely shared values and norms that confer normative legitimacy with wider publics, such as Amnesty International's support for the Universal Declaration of Human Rights. Assessing sector legitimacy involves identifying bases across sector members and articulating standards, such as respect for human rights, to which all members subscribe. Thus for IANGOs the challenge of building sector legitimacy involves considering the concerns of their constituencies and the expectations of their targets—stakeholders who often have very different expectations.

A second step in assessing sector legitimacy is to examine present challenges. Challenges are particularly problematic when they question bases at the heart of sector claims to legitimacy. When a prominent newsmagazine published articles that dismissed economic, social, and cultural rights as "wrong" and an inappropriate dilution of "more important" political and civil rights,[8] many IANGOs saw the initiative as an attack on the legitimacy of emerging economic, social, and cultural rights programs as well as a dismissal of "rights-based development" approaches to improving the lives of poor and marginalized peoples. IANGO Network members saw these articles as a direct assault on important development and advocacy concepts as well as an explicit critique of key members such as Amnesty International. Present challenges are all too easy to identify, as IANGOs that have experience with the advent of NGO Watch and media challenges to civil society advocacy can testify.

The third step of identifying potential challenges—exploring how sector legitimacy bases may be attacked or distorted in the future—may be even more important than responding to present challenges. It can be very difficult to undo damage done by challenges for which the sector is not prepared, so thinking ahead to develop preemptive or quick-response strategies is increasingly a concern for many civil society actors. The IANGO Accountability Charter, for example, is an effort to articulate the bases for sector legitimacy so that members can prepare responses to issues before they actually arise.

While sector legitimacy perceptions are often difficult to influence directly, *assessing accountability demands* can pave the way to building systems that ground legitimacy claims in responsibilities to specific stakeholders. Accountability demands focus on specific relationships among sector members and stakeholders in which expectations can be made explicit and systems for enhancing accountabilities can be constructed.

Assessing accountability demands involves identifying internal and eternal stakeholders that have accountability claims on the sector. The relationships between sectors and stakeholders are based on accountability models—agency, representative, or mutual—and on mechanisms for dealing with transparency, participation, evaluation and complaints. Different models of accountability may underlie relations with different stakeholders; for example, IANGOs emphasize mutual responsibility and accountability as key elements of relations within the Network, but they see the importance of agency and representative models with sector stakeholders as well.

As for legitimacy challenges, sector associations need to identify both present and potential accountability challenges. Present challenges make themselves known: the IANGO Network, for example, is in part a direct result of the challenges to IANGO accountability raised by NGO Watch and complaints by advocacy targets. On the other hand, potential challenges may come into view only when sector associations explore how much they are accountable to their most important stakeholders. Given the loosely organized nature of most sectors, at least before crises compel collective action, it is easy for sector members to ignore stakeholders that do not have loud voices. So analyses of potential accountability challenges may reveal discomfiting failures of accountability to important but easily ignored stakeholders. As some IANGOs grappled with identifying their accountabilities to stakeholders, for example, it became clear that enabling participation by individual members did not necessarily create accountability to victims who were not members. So careful analysis of sector accountabilities to stakeholders may expand member horizons concerning potential credibility demands and problems.

Articulating Sector Aspirations for the Future

Recognizing present and future sector challenges is important for constructing aspirations for a desired sector future. Such visions are important for motivating increased organizational credibility, and they are even more important for sector credibility when their members might prefer not to engage with the issue or with each other.

Compelling sector aspirations articulate why a more credible sector will be good for its members' missions and goals. They can also describe a theory of change that can move the sector from today's vulnerability to a future of legitimacy and strength. Without such a vision, many sector members will be inclined to go their own ways, hoping that future lightning will strike some other organization.

In the case of the IANGO Network, for example, it was important that chief executives of four influential member organizations joined the task force to create the Accountability Charter. They were keenly aware that their future influence on transnational policy making could be severely limited by a backlash that undermined public perceptions of their credibility. They had already experienced attacks on their roles as advocates. They argued that IANGOs should take the initiative to set accountability standards rather than wait for other actors to impose them. They also argued for a system that had "teeth" to enforce standards, as did the codes they advocated to regulate other sectors. Their willingness to invest their own time and resources in creating the Charter empowered others to engage in the debate and ultimately to become signatories.

Enhancing Sector Legitimacy

Chapter 4 described approaches for strengthening the legitimacy of an individual organization; these same approaches may be adapted to enhancing the legitimacy of a sector. Sector associations can also meet existing legitimacy standards and expectations by conforming to expectations, informing stakeholders about compliance, and associating with actors and activities seen as legitimate. Where current legitimacy expectations and standards limit innovation or undermine sector goals, sector leaders may also act to construct new legitimacy standards and expectations that are more appropriate.

Meeting Existing Sector Legitimacy Standards

When legitimacy expectations and standards are well established, the conforming, informing, and associating approaches to enhancing legitimacy are often effective for enhancing the sector's reputation. In the case of the newsmagazine articles that dismissed economic, social, and cultural rights as an inappropriate dilution of political and civil rights, many IANGOs saw the articles as an attack on the increasingly political work of members of the sector.

In response, several IANGOs challenged the articles as themselves being violations of existing standards of legitimacy. They wrote letters and issued press releases that highlighted misstatements of fact and shoddy arguments in the articles, informing both the general public and communicating directly with the magazine's editorial board. They also invited responses to the articles from widely respected public figures such as Mary Robinson, the former UN High Commissioner for Human Rights. They published the resulting statements from public figures on the Web sites of IANGOs mentioned in the articles. This approach combined informing wider publics with associating with eminent leaders, whose responses reinforced the importance of defining economic, social, and cultural rights as human rights.

These responses focused on legitimizing the concepts of human rights that supported the Network's development and rights-promoting activities, rather than on defending particular IANGOs. The unintended effect of the articles was to set off a firestorm of support for conceptions of economic, social, and cultural rights and rights-based development approaches. But that response depended on the vigilance of members of the IANGO Network and their ability to use their existing credibility to mobilize a rapid response to the challenge.

Constructing New Standards of Sector Legitimacy

Constructing new concepts and standards for sector legitimacy is significantly more difficult than meeting existing standards. The construction process requires articulating arguments for new standards, participating in the debates required to integrate them into existing discourses, creating new standards and expectations out of those discourses, and inventing ways to implement and assess them. Legitimizing new concepts and standards often requires engagement of many stakeholders and may involve months or years of debate to articulate standards and test their validity in practice. Nonetheless, the last few years have seen the emergence of several new sets of legitimacy and accountability standards for transnational civil society organizations, such as the Sphere Project's standards for programs of humanitarian relief organizations and the Humanitarian Accountability Project International (HAP-I), which sets standards for dealing with refugees and other vulnerable groups. In both these cases, civil society organizations have worked with other stakeholders to identify problems of legitimacy and then to create new standards to resolve those problems.

The IANGO Network seeks to strengthen sector legitimacy by creating standards and expectations though the Accountability Charter. This goal may be accomplished in part by articulating a set of standards and expectations about good practice. The document sets out general expectations that have not before been available as an explicitly transnational Charter, though most signatories have also signed national codes in their countries of origin. Establishing the standards and expectations of the Charter as credible outside the membership of the Network is more complex. Further steps include informing the world about those principles via the media, building reporting systems in collaboration with the Global Reporting Initiative, validating those systems via a multistakeholder process, and associating the Charter with similar standards articulated for corporations around the world. The construction process involves engagement across many stakeholders to create expectations that are grounded in the experience of the sector as well as in the concerns and interests of its most important stakeholders.

Building Sector Accountability Systems

Constructing sector accountability systems can be an important approach to managing legitimacy problems. The construction of sector accountability systems involves at least four elements: (1) negotiating expectations with sector stakeholders, (2) assessing and communicating sector results, (3) enabling sector performance consequences, and (4) creating sector organizations to implement the accountability system. Each of these elements is considered briefly below.

Negotiating Performance Expectations with Sector Stakeholders

Negotiating expectations enables various sector stakeholders to participate in defining the kinds of performance they can expect from sector members. These negotiations can identify areas of disagreement about expected performance and build more realistic expectations across stakeholder differences.

One set of negotiations takes place among *internal stakeholders* to define the standards of performance to which they should be held accountable. Although the discussions about the identity and goals of the sector may establish some general expectations, discussion of specific performance standards may produce difficult negotiations. Leaders of member organizations seek standards that do not disadvantage their organizations while they enhance the credibility of the sector. For example, when developing the Accountability Charter, the IANGO Network sought language that recognized differences in member strategies and tactics. Setting the expectation that sector members will respect national laws is problematic if some members use civil disobedience as an advocacy tactic and other members see unjust laws (for example, statutes that violate human rights) as a primary target. IANGO negotiations produced agreement on Charter language that emphasized advocacy that "is consistent with our mission, grounded in our work and advances defined public interests" and set expectations that members would articulate "explicit ethical policies that guide our choices of advocacy strategy."[9] Agreement on the language of the Charter is the basis for developing specific reporting standards now being drafted in cooperation with the Global Reporting Initiative.

Another set of negotiations involves *external stakeholders* that affect or are affected by sector activities, such as the IANGO stakeholders identified in Figure 6.2. The accountability assessment identifies and prioritizes sector stakeholders, while negotiating performance expectations builds agreement on how and for what the sector should be held accountable. Negotiating with sector stakeholders raises questions of conflicting demands and power differences among them. To what extent will sector negotiations pay attention to less powerful stakeholders when their interests or expectations conflict with those of more powerful actors? In discussions of the IANGO Accountability Charter, for example, it may be relatively easy to negotiate expectations with intergovernmental organizations or transnational corporations, more difficult to build agreements across scores of diverse governments, more difficult still to negotiate with (or even identify) thousands of grassroots groups that might be affected by some policies, and virtually impossible to engage with other affected stakeholders such as future generations or nonhuman populations. The IANGO Network is working with the Global Reporting Initiative to build a multistakeholder process for negotiating reporting expectations for the Accountability Charter. While this process clearly will not solve all the problems of negotiating agreed standards, it does have the advantage of using processes for setting standards that have been accepted by a wide range of corporations and governments. The IANGOs recognize that this process will be expensive and burdensome to implement, but they also recognize that enhanced legitimacy requires that IANGOs meet the kinds of standards to which they seek to hold others.

Assessing and Communicating Sector Performance Results

Sector performance expectations may include aspirational goals that are difficult to meet and minimum standards that all members are expected to attain. Assessing the extent to which sector members meet the minimum standards is critical to the credibility of the accountability system. The recent proliferation of codes of conduct for national and international civil society organizations contains several approaches to assessing compliance with sector standards.[10] Probably the most common is *member self-reports,* in which leaders self-certify that the member organization is in compliance with sector standards. InterAction, the US umbrella for international development CSOs, has used this approach for years and recently developed an elaborated self-review process.[11] Another approach is assessment by *peer review,* in which member compliance is assessed by leaders from another sector member. This approach has been extensively developed by the Philippine Council for NGO Certification to implement its Code of Conduct for Development NGOs.[12] A third assessment strategy is to organize a *complaints and redress process* that enables stakeholders to challenge the activities of members that do not live up to sector standards. This approach has been used by the Australian Council for International Development.[13] A fourth approach to assessment utilizes an *independent agency review* that assesses compliance with standards by outside evaluators. Independent reviews are relatively rare and more expensive than the other approaches, but they may also be more credible to skeptical audiences. The US child sponsorship NGOs opted for an independent review system to build a credible certification process.[14]

Communicating assessments to the relevant stakeholders may also pose challenges, particularly for transnational sectors with widely distributed stakeholders who have unequal access to information for language and technological reasons. Poor and marginalized stakeholders often have difficulty in gaining meaningful access to results. Recent initiatives have explored generating and communicating information about the performance of international relief agencies. The Human Accountability Project International has created mechanisms to allow relief recipients—often completely at the mercy of international relief organizations—to make international agencies aware of performance problems in the field in spite of their vulnerability.[15] Communicating sector results may involve annual reports or meetings with stakeholders, as is currently practiced by the Philippine Council for NGO Certification.[16] Annual reports and Web sites are also vehicles for making available information on sector performance and the outcomes of peer reviews, complaint decisions, or independent reviews.

The IANGO Charter task force has asked signatories to report their performance with respect to Charter principles during the first year of their membership. It is working with the Global Reporting Initiative to create systematic reporting requirements for the future. The task force expects to create a system to review reports and respond to complaints about member performance in the future.

Enabling Performance Consequences

Many existing sector codes of conduct use self-certification as a means of establishing member compliance. But such voluntary enforcement systems are notorious for permitting lax or fraudulent certification decisions. Many sector associations are experimenting with creating more rigorous systems for recognizing code compliance and sanctioning noncompliance. Some sectors have created complaints and redress mechanisms to identify noncompliance and sanctioned violations by revoking the memberships of noncompliers.[17] In Australia, for example, loss of membership bars offending members from taking government contracts. Others have developed peer review systems that enable review of member performance by domain peers who have strong interests in identifying and sanctioning code violations. Failure to meet peer review standards in the Philippines results in loss of tax advantages to the member's donors.[18] Still others, such as the US child sponsorship organizations, have invested in independent third-party certification of their compliance with standards. Success in the certification process allows the member to display a "seal of approval" that is expected to help substantially in fundraising appeals.[19] Systems for enabling performance consequences have to be designed with an eye to issues such as the likelihood of noncompliance, the skepticism of external stakeholders, and the resources available to support expensive regulation processes.

Many IANGOs have been critical of "voluntary" codes of conduct for regulating businesses and governments since they have seen how easy it is to abuse voluntary standards. There was much debate in early discussions of the Accountability Charter about the need for mechanisms to identify and sanction violations. The signatories reluctantly recognized that the Charter requires serious enforcement mechanisms to establish its own credibility. Members have agreed that some sort of complaints and redress system will be required, in which an ombudsman or an independent committee reviews complaints about signatory noncompliance. But members are also aware that the domain includes many small and informal networks that will have difficulty meeting elaborate Charter requirements, so they expect to develop graduated mechanisms that recognize the realities of diverse member resources and stages of development.

Creating Sector Organizations to Implement Accountability Systems

Sector accountability systems typically require ongoing attention and resources, even when they assign large amounts of responsibility to their members. When sectors are initially defined in response to credibility challenges, as was the IANGO Network, creating the organizational resources to administer an accountability system may be a significant challenge. Implementing and maintaining a domain accountability system can be a substantial task, particularly if the domain has many members who engage in controversial activities. Effective sector accountability systems may require investing considerable time, energy, and resources to register members, review reports, manage complaints and certification issues, and revise systems in response to emerging issues. While sector associations often serve as secretariats for registration, reviewing reports and managing complaints or conflicts may require more neutrality and credibility than is feasible for associations that are organized to serve their members. So creating sector accountability systems may require new organizational arrangements that are seen as neutral and unbiased by external stakeholders.

The IANGO Network is an example of a newly defined sector that emerged from workshops to create the Accountability Charter. Rather than create a new organization, the Network asked the CIVICUS Worldwide Alliance for Citizen Participation, one of the original conveners of the IANGO Workshop, to become the secretariat for the Network and for the Accountability Charter. As secretariat for the Network, CIVICUS organizes and facilitates the annual IANGO workshop; as secretariat for the Charter it manages the Charter website, maintains a membership roster, and provides administrative support for signatories of the Charter. The Charter task force is working with the Global Reporting Initiative to develop a reporting system and is also developing proposals for investigating and adjudicating complaints. This task will probably require creating an independent Charter Committee to deal with complaints and redress. It has become clear that new organizational arrangements will be required to implement and sustain the emerging Charter.

Using Sector Accountability Systems

Creating sector accountability systems is emerging as an increasingly common response to criticism of a sector's existence and activities. When credible sector accountability systems are developed and negotiated with the relevant stakeholders, they can be used for multiple purposes, several of which are described below.

Strengthening Sector Legitimacy and Support

Sector accountability systems are designed to enhance the accountability and legitimacy of the sector. Members can point to the system and their compliance with its standards in response to legitimacy questions. Ideally, accountability systems give specific and credible answers to questions about "who is accountable to whom for what and how?" They also indicate how dissatisfied stakeholders can hold sector members accountable to minimum standards and expectations. Critics of the activities of particular IANGO signatories to the Accountability Charter gained an arena in which to make their cases.

For sector members, constructing an accountability system calls for clarifying the nature of the sector and its contributions to advancing public value. The process offers members an opportunity to join with other similar organizations to define core values and responsibilities, and so to shape the tests against which the sector will be measured in the future. While the members cannot dictate what other stakeholders will conclude about the value of their goals and the legitimacy of the sector, they can play active roles in generating arguments and integrating their perspectives into discourses about sector values, roles, and activities. To the extent that the articulation of sector identity and aspirations resonates with the concerns of larger publics, creating accountability systems may enhance the sector's legitimacy and visibility as a social force as well as the availability of support for its ongoing activities. Information from sector accountability systems may be used to expand support from interested donors and regulators, particularly if they have been included in negotiating sector expectations. The deliberations of the IANGO Network and the development of the Accountability Charter generated considerable public interest and media coverage. The initiative has contributed to widespread interest in the issues of accountability and legitimacy among civil society organizations all over the world.

Building Sector Operational Capacity

The construction of sector accountability systems may also be used to enhance sector operational capabilities. Agreement on standards and information about how to meet them can increase sector understanding of good practices and effective responses to common challenges. The identification of performance concerns across the sector can sensitize members to common problems and risks and spread information about effective practices and problem solutions. The effort to define and operationalize Accountability Charter standards and expectations is pressing IANGOs as a community to understand more about the operational challenges of advocacy in transnational contexts.

The creation of sector arrangements to implement accountability systems can also enhance the capacity of the sector for collective action in the face of other problems. The experience of creating the Accountability Charter has expanded membership in the IANGO Network, as other IANGOs have decided they want to participate in the construction and implementation of the Charter. The success of the Charter as an innovation has also enhanced Network members' willingness and capacity to build coalitions and shared initiatives on other problems, such as climate change and relations with corporations.

Creating Sector Value

Creating and using a sector accountability system also offers opportunities for sector strategic learning to achieve widely held goals and aspirations. Debates and discourses on concepts that shape common sector strategies and tactics may have profound effects on how members define and pursue goals and objectives. Membership in an emerging domain that brings together many diverse perspectives that can catalyze new thinking among members. In the arena of transnational governance and problem solving, for example, such new perspectives may be very important for enabling social learning and change.

The engagement of transnational advocacy organizations and networks concerned with many different issues in the IANGO Network, for example, provides many opportunities for stimulating new ideas and alliances. Discussions across the environmental, human rights, and poverty alleviation traditions has fostered discussion of concepts, such as "sustainable rights-based development," that draw on all three traditions. Engagement across historically separate advocacy issues has emphasized how many issues (e.g., rights violations, poverty, and environmental degradation) converge to affect the poorest and most disenfranchised populations. Recognition of convergence has sparked more discussion of building cross-issue alliances. As newly defined sectors bring together old antagonists or join previously unconnected perspectives, engagement across differences can spark new concepts and change theories within and across sectors.[20]

Catalyzing Wider Discourses

The arguments and discourses stimulated by sector credibility issues often reverberate beyond the sector. Some debates are at the tip of large icebergs, and discourses within sectors cannot define legitimacy and accountability standards without involving other sectors. As IANGO leaders prepared to launch the Accountability Charter at a press conference, some of them pointed out that once the initiative was launched, there would be no turning back. The failure to create an accountability system would have high costs in credibility for signatories and for international civil society in general. Once in the public eye, many forces would demand development of the Charter as a strong set of enforceable standards.

The values, standards, and expectations that grow out of struggles over legitimacy and accountability will constrain and enable critical encounters for decades. Communities separated by enormous gaps in wealth and resources, radically inconsistent political systems, and fundamental differences in values and cultural perspectives are being dragged willy-nilly into mutual awareness and interdependence by global markets and expanding information flows. It is not a coincidence that these credibility issues emerge so clearly in the international arena. Lack of shared authority and common regulations, prevalence of poorly understood problems, and large differences in values and aspirations create fertile grounds for misunderstanding and challenge to legitimacy and accountability.

The construction of sector accountability systems offers opportunities to engage with many stakeholders to negotiate mutual understanding and agreements about legitimacy and accountability standards. Those engagements can articulate or change standards for legitimacy for civil society sectors that shape their activities in transnational arenas. IANGOs that violate the Accountability Charter may not yet be sanctioned for those violations, but they can no longer easily plead ignorance. Social and political construction processes shape the standards and expectations of other sectors as well. When corporations and governments join multistakeholder processes to set standards for IANGOs, they also influence the standards that will be applied to their own activities in the future. The IANGOs are creating an Accountability Charter "with teeth" because they want credibility with their corporate and government targets, but they are also contributing to setting expectations for those other sectors in the process.

The dynamics of sector accountability system construction can be self-reinforcing. As more influential IANGOs sign on to the Charter, it becomes more difficult for others to justify not signing. Sector critics will point out the Charter's inadequacies and shortcomings and create pressure for remedying them. At the same time, compliance with the Charter strengthens member credibility to demand compliance from their advocacy targets. This gives the Charter the potential to increase the power of legitimacy regimes more generally. Correspondingly, there are also significant risks: failure to comply can produce member, stakeholder, and public cynicism about sector credibility and thus catalyze a self-reinforcing downward spiral in the capacity of IANGOs to hold themselves or others accountable.

Summary

This chapter began by discussing the rise in questions about the credibility of sector domains—communities of organizations with similar strategies and activities. It focused on assessing sector legitimacy and accountability, arguing that such assessments should define the nature and composition of the sector, identify primary goals and strategies, map and prioritize its internal and external stakeholders, assess its legitimacy and accountability challenges, and articulate sector aspirations for the future. On the basis of that assessment, sector leaders may enhance sector legitimacy by meeting existing expectations and standards or by constructing new ones that better fit sector values and goals. The assessment can also be the basis for constructing sector accountability systems. That construction involves negotiating stakeholder performance expectations, assessing and communicating performance results, enabling good and bad performance consequences, and creating organizational arrangements to implement and sustain the accountability system.

Finally the chapter turned to the use of sector accountability systems. The information they produce can be used to enhance sector legitimacy and support, build increased sector capacity, and increase sector value creation in various ways. Arguments and debates over sector accountability systems can contribute to creating standards for other sectors as well. The stakes of the transnational drama over legitimacy and accountability may be larger than the obvious risks for civil society sectors and their stakeholders. The intersectoral struggle over legitimacy and accountability in a few domains may shape the future of international engagements on many fronts.

Notes

1. It is short of ideal to use the term "sector" to mean both "activity sector" in the sense of child sponsorship and human rights sectors and "institutional sector" in the sense of the business, government and civil society sectors. Both uses of the term are quite common, however. I have tried to recognize the dual meanings rather than create new terms that reflect the differences more clearly.

2. Florini, Ann, *The Third Force: The Rise of Transnational Civil Society* (New York: Carnegie Endowment for International Peace, 2000): 9. See also Fisher, Julie, *The Road from Rio: Sustainable Development and the Non-governmental Movement in the Third World* (New York: Praeger, 1993); and Hawken, Paul, *Blessed Unrest: How the Largest Movement in the World Came into Being and Why No One Saw It Coming* (New York: Viking, 2007).

3. The author has convened and facilitated these meetings in cooperation with colleagues from the Hauser Center for Nonprofit

Organizations at Harvard and the CIVICUS Worldwide Alliance for Citizen Participation. Information for the discussion of this case has been gathered from participant observation in the course of this work.

4. Brown, L. David and Jagadananda, "Civil Society Legitimacy and Accountability: Issues and Challenges," (Johannesburg: CIVICUS World Alliance for Citizen Participation, 2007).

5. See Phillips, M., "Big Charities Pursue Certification to Quell Fears of Funding Abuses," *Wall Street Journal*, March 9, 2005; and Scott, Esther, "Standards for Child Sponsorship Agencies (A)," Kennedy School of Government Case C16-02-1664.0, 2002.

6. See Gray, B. G., *Collaborating: Finding Common Ground for Multiparty Problems* (San Francisco: Jossey-Bass, 1989); and Weber, Edward, *Bringing Society Back In: Grassroots Ecosystem Management, Accountability and Sustainable Communities* (Cambridge, MA: MIT Press, 2003).

7. Brown, L. David and Moore, Mark H., "Accountability, Strategy and International Nongovernmental Organizations," *Nonprofit and Voluntary Sector Quarterly*, 30, no. 3 (2001): 569–587.

8. "Stand up for your rights," *The Economist*, vol. 382, issue 8521, March 24, 2007.

9. See International Nongovernmental Organisations Accountability Charter, p. 3, at http://www.ingoaccountabilitycharter.org/principles.html (retrieved August 22, 2007).

10. See Lloyd, Robert, *The Role of NGO Self-Regulation in Increasing Stakeholder Accountability* (London: One World Trust, 2005).

11. See InterAction PVO Standards at http://www.interaction.org/pvostandards/index.html (retrieved August 22, 2007).

12. Chamberlain, R. A., *Regulating Civil Society: The Philippine Council for NGO Certification*, (Manila: PCNC, 1998). Also see PCNC website at www.pcnc.com.ph.

13. See the Australian Council for International Development Code of Conduct monitoring provisions at http://www.acfid.asn.au/code-of-conduct/complaints-and-compliance-monitoring (retrieved August 22, 2007).

14. Phillips, M., "Big Charities Pursue Certification to Quell Fears of Funding Abuses," *Wall Street Journal*, March 9, 2005.

15. For information about the Human Accountability Project, see Callamard, A., "HAP International: A New Decisive Step toward Accountability," *AccountAbility Forum*, 2 (2004): 44–57, and for additional information: http://www.hapinternational.org.

16. Chamberlain, *Regulating Civil Society* (1998). Also see PCNC Web site at www.pcnc.com.ph.

17. See Lloyd, "The Role of NGO Self-Regulation in Increasing Stakeholder Accountability" (2005).

18. See Chamberlain, *Regulating Civil Society* (1998).

19. Phillips, "Big Charities Pursue Certification to Quell Fears of Funding Abuses" (2005).

20. Brown, L. David and Timmer, Vanessa, "Transnational Civil Society and Social Learning," *Voluntas: International Journal of Voluntary and Nonprofit Organizations*, 17, no. 1 (2006): 1–16; Nelson, Paul, and Dorsey, Ellen, "At the Nexus of Human Rights and Development: New Methods and Strategies of Global NGOs," *World Development*, 31, no. 12 (2003): 2013–2026.

Negotiating Campaign Credibility

When the Philippine government decided to build a thermal power plant at the top of Mount Apo, it was responding to the escalating national demand for electric power. But the decision set off strong reactions among local farmers, environmental NGOs, and indigenous peoples for whom Mount Apo was sacred. These groups launched a campaign to stop the plant that eventually involved litigation in the country's highest courts, initiatives to rescind World Bank financing, civil disobedience to stop plant construction, and initiatives to block other international support for the project. The campaign's effectiveness turned on building its credibility across a wide range of local, regional, national, and international actors.

Negotiating credibility in a sector domain involves organizations that carry out similar activities and the stakeholders of those organizations. Sector members may have histories of competition or conflict, but they often have similar appreciations of the world and their roles in it. Negotiating credibility in a *campaign domain* requires building agreements across what may be dramatic differences in perspective and interests. Campaign allies may have very different missions and interests outside of the particular campaign. The farmer organizations, development NGOs, environmental activists, and indigenous peoples' groups brought very different perspectives and interests to the Mount Apo campaign. Campaign allies often operate at different societal levels and so bring diverse concerns, resources, and statuses to the campaign: grassroots farmer organizations and indigenous groups in the rural Philippines are very different from international environment or development NGOs headquartered in Washington, D.C. But building campaign coalitions across such differences in power and perspective is critical to the David-and-Goliath encounters in which local interests and coalitions seek to influence projects defined by national governments or the World Bank. Managing power inequalities is at the heart of the internal dynamics of campaign coalitions, and it is pivotal to their success in influencing transnational institutions and decision makers.

This chapter focuses on the challenges of negotiating legitimacy and accountability expectations in transnational advocacy campaigns. It proposes approaches to strengthening legitimacy and enabling accountability to key stakeholders internal and external to the campaign. As in earlier chapters, this chapter will consider four aspects of the problem: (1) assessing the legitimacy and accountability challenges facing the campaign, (2) enhancing campaign legitimacy, (3) constructing campaign accountability systems, and (4) using those systems to advance the campaign's mission and strategy. The Mount Apo campaign is used to illustrate the challenges and possibilities of constructing legitimacy and accountability systems to influence international projects and institutions.[1]

Assessing Campaign Legitimacy and Accountability

Campaigns are interorganizational coalitions organized around shared goals and analyses to advocate with decision makers. They are often more focused on particular goals and more time-limited than sector associations. Civil society–led campaigns sometimes emerge in response to initiatives that directly affect marginalized populations, as in the case of the Mount Apo initiative or the campaigns to stop the Narmada Dam construction. On other occasions they may be organized around more general policy decisions, such as the international campaign against landmines or the campaign to reduce the debt owed by developing countries.[2] As for other interorganizational domains, the definition of the campaign is itself an important element of developing an assessment of campaign legitimacy and accountability systems. We focus here on (1) defining campaign issues and convening potential members, (2) articulating campaign missions, strategies, and goals, (3) mapping internal and external stakeholders, (4) assessing legitimacy and accountability demands, and (5) constructing aspirations for the future.

Defining Campaign Issues and Convening Members

Campaigns are usually temporary systems, organized around specific issues and goals that provide compelling reasons for members to surrender some organizational autonomy in order to achieve shared goals that they cannot achieve alone. For such campaigns, several issues are important. First, framing campaign issues so that they touch critical interests and provide a base for mobilizing energy from key constituents is central. If constituents do not see the issues as vital, it will be hard to persuade policymakers that they should pay attention. Second, the nature and reputation of campaign conveners are central to bringing allies into the coalition. Conveners who are seen as credible, trustworthy, and effective in accomplishing campaign goals are important resources in getting the necessary participants involved.

The Mount Apo campaign was set off by initial survey work that signaled the government's intention to build the thermal plant. That activity drew the attention of the local indigenous peoples, since it involved drilling pilot holes on sacred lands. It also became a concern for local farmers' organizations and environmental activists worried about its ecological consequences. Church organizations and many other activists concerned with vulnerable groups in the Philippines were also active participants in the early discussions. Previous government projects, many carried out with funding from outside agencies such as the World Bank, had often been implemented with little attention to the interests of low-power stakeholders. So the initial mobilization of local groups was soon supported by coalitions at the regional and national levels.

From the start, conveners of the local alliance were people with basic interests at stake: Indigenous peoples' associations, for example, used the earlier campaign by indigenous groups against the Chico River Dam to rally support for protecting the sacred lands on Mount Apo. Farmer associations and environmental activists had been sensitized by environmental damage created by earlier power projects. The Catholic Church had been in the forefront of many initiatives to protect marginalized groups in the Philippines and so was trusted by many social activists. Civil society actors in the Philippines had a substantial history of alliance building across issues and levels, so the social and institutional capital to support a campaign on the Mount Apo issue was already available. But recognizing mutual interests in stopping a project is only a first step; building more specific definitions of the problem and strategies for action takes more investment.

Defining Campaign Missions, Strategies, and Goals

Although defining missions and strategies may be relatively easy for organizations, considerable discussion and debate are often required to construct missions, strategies, and goals for multiorganization campaigns. It is uncommon for members to share problem analyses, agree on campaign missions, or develop consensus on strategies for accomplishing those missions at the outset of a campaign. It is more common for such agreements to emerge from weeks, months, or years of discussion; engagement with opponents; and exploration of alternatives. Choice of mission and strategy typically involves ongoing negotiations among campaign members and subcoalitions.

A modified strategic triangle can be applied to thinking about the elements of a campaign strategy. Understanding multiorganization campaigns requires attention to relations among campaign members and their contributions to value creation, legitimacy and support, and operational

Figure 7.1 Campaign Strategic Triangle

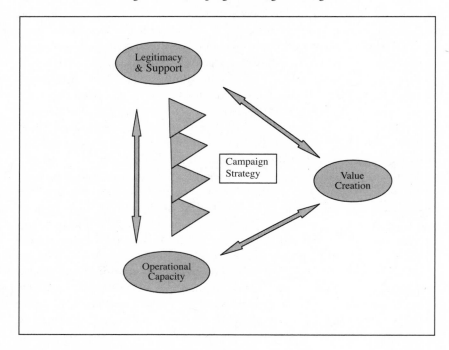

capacity issues. Figure 7.1 reflects the participation of campaign coalition members oriented to creating the same value (reflected by their right apexes all pointing in the same direction) but concerned about legitimacy and support and operational capacity at different levels of analysis. The overlap of the gray triangles suggests that the members of the campaign may contribute to enhancing each other's legitimacy and support and to building the operational capacity of the larger campaign. Overall, the campaign may mobilize resources and capacities that significantly outweigh those available to its individual members.

Building a campaign strategy involves decisions about the value to be created, the legitimacy and support the campaign requires, and the operational capacity needed to accomplish its goals. Value creation includes goals such as changing a specific policy, building capacity for influencing decision making, or creating precedents for grassroots voices to be heard in decisions that affect them. Different goals may imply different campaign targets, legitimacy-building strategies, and required operational capacities. Policy campaigns can utilize various forms of advocacy strategy, such as education, persuasion, litigation, or contestation, to influence targets and accomplish campaign goals. The choice of advocacy strategies also has implications for legitimacy and support and for operational capacity.

The Mount Apo campaign, for example, focused on stopping the project by influencing several targets. The immediate target was the government of the Philippines, and in particular the agencies involved in building power plants. When those agencies proved difficult to influence, the lawyer allies of the campaign challenged the project in national courts. At the same time, international campaign members sought to influence the World Bank, which was providing economic and political support seen as critical to the project's viability. When efforts with government agencies and the courts failed, the campaign focused on getting the Bank to withdraw its support as a way to dissuade the Philippine government from going forward.

Agreement on strategy only emerged over considerable time and extensive debate within the campaign coalition. The coalition participants each had different agendas: the indigenous peoples sought to protect the sacred lands, environmentalists were worried about ecological conservation, farmers and consumer organizations were concerned about the plant impacts on the watershed, church and human rights activists were concerned about preserving due process, and other participants wanted to challenge government and World Bank policies.[3] Clear agreement on emphasizing the rights of indigenous peoples to preserve their sacred lands emerged several years after the campaign began, when local, regional, and national activists began meeting in "national solidarity councils" to assess progress and debate alternative approaches. These debates enabled the construction of shared campaign mission and strategies grounded in better understanding of the concerns of campaign participants, the areas in which public support favored the campaign, and the interests and commitments of potential allies such as World Bank policymakers. Such ongoing discourses and debates create more widely shared frames and stories for building wider public support for campaign positions.

The evolution of campaign missions and strategies is shaped by the influence of internal and external stakeholders. Philippine members of the Mount Apo campaign were concerned that international members, such as the Philippine Development Forum (PDF) in Washington, would use their access to the World Bank to pursue their own interests rather than those of the local constituencies. The relative capacities of indigenous peoples' groups and environmental activists to influence campaign targets were also the subject of much discussion. Defining missions and strategies across campaigns may take a long time and a lot of effort compared to organizational strategic choices—but it can also mobilize the energies and resources of a wide range of participants.

Mapping and Prioritizing Campaign Stakeholders

Campaigns often have more diverse stakeholders than do sectors, since campaign members come from different fields and levels to work together for shared interests in campaign missions and goals. Campaigns are also especially concerned with influencing powerful external stakeholders or policy targets, so influence dynamics and power relations are central concerns in actions inside and outside the coalition.

Figure 7.2 indicates some of the stakeholders that were important to the Mount Apo campaign. Internal stakeholders, such as local, regional, national, and international coalition members, are represented by the linked gray triangles at the center of the figure. External stakeholders concerned with value creation, legitimacy and support, and operational capacity are represented in the ovals clustered around each apex.

Internal stakeholders share interests in the campaign focus, but they often bring different perspectives, information, and resources. Defining and implementing performance and accountability expectations can be very difficult before campaign members agree on a shared mission and

Figure 7.2 Mount Apo Campaign Stakeholders

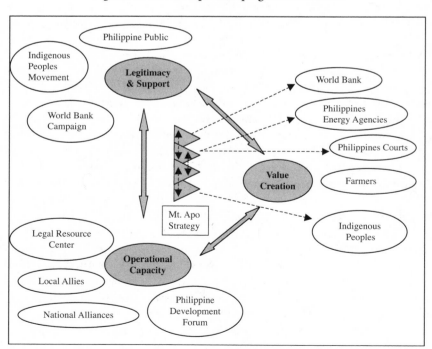

strategy. Even after agreement, the differences in power and resources among internal stakeholders can make negotiation of specific expectations problematic. Experience with multilevel alliances suggests that accountability relationships are more easily created across adjacent levels (see the dotted arrows in Figure 7.2 linking internal stakeholders) than across the multiple levels that separate grassroots members from international actors.[4] In the Mount Apo campaign, the national solidarity councils grappled with building relations of trust and mutual accountability among local, regional, and national allies. Those national councils continued to be skeptical about the role and activities of the PDF, which as an international partner provided access to World Bank officials in Washington. But the PDF had been encouraged to liaise with the Bank before the national solidarity councils were created and a shared strategy was formulated. So other members of the campaign worked to construct informal expectations about how the PDF would remain accountable to the campaign as a whole.

External stakeholders for value creation included both clients (local indigenous peoples, farmers) and targets (government energy agencies, national courts, the World Bank). Campaign members at different levels vary in their positioning and expertise to work with different targets: the dashed arrows suggest that local members are better able to work with local indigenous groups and farmers, national members are better positioned to influence national government agencies, and international allies are better positioned to influence the World Bank. Credibility with external stakeholders often turns on the capacity of the campaign to work effectively across levels. The World Bank, for example, often asks international groups such as the PDF to demonstrate how they actually represent and are accountable to grassroots constituents. So the link across the chasms that separate Washington advocates from indigenous peoples on the slopes of Mount Apo became critical to campaign credibility with key policy targets.

Evolving strategies may change the priority of internal and external campaign stakeholders. Campaign events or shifting external contexts may redefine the importance and roles of important actors. In the Mount Apo campaign, for example, shifting public concerns and policymaker awareness focused attention in the Philippines and at the World Bank on the rights of indigenous peoples, and the campaign increased emphasis on indigenous rights to take advantage of that attention. Mapping and prioritization of stakeholders may evolve to adapt to shifting internal and external contexts.

Assessing Campaign Legitimacy and Accountability Demands

Assessing the legitimacy demands of campaigns depends on their missions and goals. For most advocacy campaigns, the important bases of legitimacy include political legitimacy from representing important constituents, associational legitimacy based on credible members and allies, perform-ance legitimacy from information and resources that are important to cam-paign targets, and normative legitimacy from their support of widely shared values and norms. Regulatory legitimacy may also be important when the campaign presses policymakers to live up to their own regulations and poli-cies, as in many campaigns to influence World Bank projects. Cognitive legitimacy is not irrelevant to campaigns, but such campaigns often operate in areas where cognitive expectations are confused or not well established.

Some demands are reflected in *current legitimacy challenges.* For cam-paign leaders, dealing with immediate challenges takes precedence over many potential future challenges. For example, the government of the Philippines challenged the legitimacy of the Mount Apo campaign in sev-eral ways. The government argued that the need for increased energy resources—especially nonpolluting resources such as thermal energy—preempted the claims of special-interest groups such as the indigenous peoples. It challenged the legitimacy of the indigenous elders, who had vowed to die rather than permit violation of their sacred lands, by spon-soring counter-declarations and counter-ceremonials by rival indigenous leaders. It also questioned the campaign's credibility with World Bank staff members who were being lobbied by the campaign to withdraw sup-port from the Mount Apo plant.

The Mount Apo campaign emphasized the political legitimacy of rep-resenting the interests of the indigenous people and their elected leaders. The campaign drew on the normative legitimacy rooted in the national commitment to respect the rights of indigenous peoples. The support of the Catholic Church conferred both associational and normative legiti-macy in a predominantly Catholic country. The campaign also sought reg-ulatory legitimacy for its claims by arguing that the government was violating its own laws.

Campaign leaders can also predict *potential legitimacy challenges* that may be raised in the future by reflecting on the kinds of legitimacy that are or could be mobilized to support campaign goals and activities. It was clear to the Mount Apo campaign leaders that legitimacy was critical to its abil-ity to affect targets such as the Supreme Court, government energy agen-cies, and the World Bank. Within the campaign there was much debate about whether it should emphasize the environmental destruction wrought by the proposed plant, its impacts on local farmers, or its viola-tion of the rights of indigenous peoples to their sacred lands. Eventually the campaign focused on the latter, in part because the issue had become widely discussed and debated in the Philippines and at the World Bank. The public concern with indigenous rights persuaded campaign strate-gists to use that frame for the campaign's goals and its associated legiti-macy with both the larger public and the World Bank.

Assessing the accountability demands of a campaign focuses attention on relations among campaign members and on the campaign's relations with specific external stakeholders. Again, leaders may focus on either current or potential accountability claims. The emphasis on indigenous peoples' rights helped clarify the importance of the campaign's internal accountability to indigenous leaders. Its legitimacy with World Bank staff, for example, depended on how much it actually represented and was accountable to indigenous leaders. The debates about goals and strategies in national solidarity councils helped to create mutual accountability across levels and among diverse members of the international coalition. Since agency contracts or voter mandates were not easily available to the coalition, negotiated mutual accountability became an important basis for joint planning and action. Debates about goals and strategies created performance expectations on which mutual accountability could be based.

Campaign analysis of missions, strategies, and stakeholders can clarify the accountability claims that might be made by different stakeholders. In the Mount Apo campaign, the centrality of the indigenous peoples required more campaign attention to their concerns than those of conservationists or farmers or church leaders, even though all those groups wanted to block completion of the plant. So changing goals and strategies may have important implications for which stakeholders have priority and which accountabilities are most important.

Articulating Aspirations for the Future

Campaigns are often actors with limited futures, at least in comparison to organizations and sectors, because their aspirations are often closely tied to the accomplishment of short-term objectives such as campaign policy goals. The Mount Apo campaign, for example, focused on stopping the power plant project, and it framed aspirations for legitimacy and accountability in terms of that struggle. Since legitimacy and accountability in the eyes of targets and wider publics can be critical to campaign credibility and effectiveness, campaign leaders face powerful incentives to achieve short-term legitimacy and accountability aspirations. But in the pressures of day-to-day campaigning they are also pressed to respond to the latest moves of their opponents rather than to think about the longer term. Leaders of the Mount Apo campaign coordinated a wide variety of activities, from court cases to pubic demonstrations to media events to World Bank visits, and they faced a wide range of government initiatives and responses.

On the other hand, research suggests that civil society policy campaigns can have impacts well beyond their immediate policy consequences.

Comparative research in the Philippines, for example, indicated that campaigns also contributed to enhancing or eroding the capacities of their members and to shaping the national reputation of civil society policy initiatives.[5] The incentives for articulating longer-term aspirations for campaign credibility seldom rival the demands for credibility that affect immediate campaign outcomes. But highly visible campaigns provide critical examples of legitimacy and accountability (or illegitimacy and unaccountability) that shape the contexts of future campaigns. The Mount Apo campaign, for example, has probably strengthened the hand of indigenous organizations in future efforts to protect their rights in the Philippines, though that was not an explicit goal of the campaign. So campaign leaders with a longer-term perspective will think about the wider implications of current strategies and tactics and set aspirations for the campaign that strengthen their future credibility as well as their immediate impact on decisions.

Enhancing Campaign Legitimacy

Legitimacy with campaign targets or with publics that influence those targets is pivotal to campaign success, so responding to legitimacy challenges that affect those targets and publics can be critical. Decisions about goals and strategy can shape the areas in which challenges are likely to emerge: focusing on indigenous peoples' rights in the Mount Apo campaign increased the likelihood of efforts to undermine the legitimacy of indigenous elders, just as focusing on environmental problems might increase efforts to challenge the scientific basis of predicted environmental consequences.

Legitimacy springs from widespread perceptions of the value and appropriateness of the campaign's goals and behavior, and so it cannot be easily negotiated with particular stakeholders. When transnational campaigns frame new problems in underregulated arenas, however, they operate where legitimacy standards are not well established. Campaign members can articulate their goals and implement their activities in terms that draw on various sources of legitimacy. Advocacy campaigns can make use of the performance value of participant expertise, the political value of representing affected constituents, the normative value of framing goals that express and preserve widely held norms and values, the associational value of recruiting widely reputable members, and the cognitive value of congruence between campaigns and widely held social expectations. As in prior analyses, initiatives to enhance legitimacy can focus on demonstrating campaign fit with existing legitimacy standards or on constructing new standards that are more appropriate to the campaign and emerging circumstances.

Demonstrating Compliance with Existing Campaign Standards

Demonstrating compliance with existing standards is usually an easier case to make. Campaigns can argue that they comply with existing regulations and that their targets do not. The Mount Apo campaign argued that that government was violating its own regulations about preserving indigenous peoples' rights to control their land. The campaign actively informed the wider public about its normative legitimacy in terms of widely held values and its political representation of indigenous groups. It explicitly attacked government efforts to undermine the legitimacy of tribal elders opposed to the plant. (The government had been sponsoring and publicizing the views of nonrepresentative indigenous "leaders" who supported the creation of the plant.) The campaign explicitly built its associational legitimacy by building linkages with a wide range of other actors such as the Catholic Church and international NGOs and networks.

Most campaigns must demonstrate legitimacy in terms of existing standards in order to attract members and build a credible alliance. Articulating missions and goals and demonstrating bases for legitimacy that justify the campaign to a wider public are prerequisites to launching a campaign. The Mount Apo campaign was able to mobilize members by appealing to concerns around which constituents—farmers, environmentalists, Catholic activists, and indigenous peoples—were already organized. But in some cases campaigns may also have to create new or altered standards of legitimacy to achieve their goals.

Constructing New Campaign Standards

Constructing new standards and frameworks for legitimacy is a challenging and time-consuming strategy. On the other hand, campaigns can make good use of evolving debates and discourses that are relevant to their members. The Mount Apo campaign, for example, recognized that both the government of the Philippines and the World Bank were grappling with questions about the rights of indigenous peoples. Those issues were also alive for wider publics in the Philippines. So focusing the campaign on indigenous rights, rather than on farmer or environmentalist concerns, placed the campaign at the center of emerging national and international debates. That choice enhanced the power of the campaign in the national context, it reframed the problem from energy development to indigenous rights at the World Bank, and it enhanced the power of the indigenous leaders as stakeholders within the campaign.

Legitimacy in campaigns involves grappling with power differences within the campaign across member levels and interests as well as overcoming power differences between the campaign and its targets. The creation of accountability systems that define expectations for performance among members and between the campaign and its external stakeholders can be critical for enhancing legitimacy.

Constructing Campaign Accountability Systems

The assessment of accountability claims provides the basis for constructing improved systems for meeting accountability expectations, which in turn can enhance the campaign's legitimacy. Constructing accountability systems involves (1) negotiating stakeholder expectations, (2) creating performance measurements, (3) enabling performance consequences, and (4) organizing to implement accountability systems for an advocacy strategy that operates across levels and power differences.

Negotiating Stakeholder Expectations

Building accountability systems focuses on articulating specific expectations of stakeholders who have plausible claims on campaign performance. Enhancing the capacity of the campaign to meet the accountability expectations of internal stakeholders, such as campaign members, and external stakeholders, such as constituents or wider publics, can strengthen its claims to wider legitimacy.

Internal stakeholders share commitments to campaign goals and strategies and depend on each other to implement campaign strategies. While many campaigns begin with very general goals, successful campaigns often develop complex and detailed activities to deal with the evolving challenges of policy influence. Implementing plans through a coalition of diverse organizations is very difficult if responsibilities are not explicit and members cannot be trusted to carry them out. Campaign participants must negotiate performance expectations and hold each other accountable for implementing them. Mutual accountability based on shared values and relationships is more common as a model for accountability in civil society campaigns than the models of democratic representation or principal-agent relations. But whatever the underlying model, agreeing about performance and holding members accountable are both important to campaign success.

The Mount Apo campaign gradually evolved an increasingly detailed and widely shared strategy that spelled out expectations for local, regional, national, and international members. The national solidarity meetings were particularly concerned with maintaining control over the Washington-based PDF and its representation of the campaign at the World Bank. The meetings focused attention on the PDF: visits by the

PDF coordinator to the indigenous elders on Mount Apo built a personal bond that enabled mutual accountability with the grassroots level of the campaign.

The Mount Apo campaign also sought legitimacy with campaign targets such as the government energy agencies, the national courts, and the World Bank, as well as other external stakeholders, such as the wider Philippine public or indigenous peoples' movements. While it is not clear that the government of the Philippines ever accepted the legitimacy of the Mount Apo campaign, the national courts gave the campaign standing to challenge the government's actions, and the World Bank came to rely on the campaign for information about the concerns of the indigenous peoples. The Bank's acceptance of the campaign depended on its continued legitimacy with and accountability to the indigenous peoples' leaders.

The capacity of campaigns to negotiate with external stakeholders often evolves over time as campaigns build legitimacy with powerful parties that paid little attention at the outset. The Philippines energy agencies initially ignored the Mount Apo campaign, but as support for the indigenous peoples' rights mounted, the government encouraged efforts to mobilize "alternative" sets of elders to undermine the campaign. The willingness of the original elders to sustain their commitment to the campaign depended in part on their belief in the campaign's accountability to indigenous groups. Negotiating stakeholder expectations depends in part on a campaign's ability to gain the visibility and influence that make it a plausible participant in the advocacy process.

Assessing and Communicating Results

The performance of advocacy campaigns can be framed in several ways. While sector standards are often created to measure repeated activities of sector members, campaigns are often tailored to unique constellations of circumstances and actions. For this reason, regular peer- or independent-review mechanisms are less useful than assessments tailored to particular campaign goals and strategies. The immediate objectives of advocacy campaigns often emphasize changing the policies or practices of specific target agencies, though they may have wider goals for members or the larger system as well. The assessment of performance may be couched in terms of assessing impacts, constructing stories, or analyzing institutional results.

Impact assessment requires articulating a change theory that explains how campaign activities will produce outputs that catalyze changed behavior by clients or targets, which will in turn produce longer-term impacts consistent with campaign goals. In the Mount Apo campaign, for example, campaign outputs included legal and policy analyses, public demonstrations, and briefings for World Bank officials. These outputs enabled outcomes in changed behavior of key actors, such as public expressions of concern about the campaign and indigenous peoples' rights, decisions against supporting the project by the World Bank and other financial institutions, and long delays in project development. The longer-term impacts of the campaign included enhanced legitimacy of the indigenous peoples' movement in the Philippines, enhanced reputation of civil society alliances with the World Bank, and increased organizational capacity for policy campaigns among members. Campaign change theories that link outputs to outcomes, and outcomes to impacts, enable them to focus on activities and stakeholders that are critical to desired changes. The Mount Apo campaign, for example, did not persuade the government to abandon its plans in the short term, but it did delay the plant and influence financing by the World Bank and other international sources.

Story construction focuses on articulating the values, history, and impacts of campaigns in terms that help members and supporters understand their meaning and commit to future initiatives. While the audience for impact analysis often consists of donors or political scientists, the audience for stories consists of campaign activists and the wider public. In the Mount Apo campaign, the ceremonial commitment of the indigenous elders to die rather than to give up their sacred lands converged with increasing national concern about the fate of indigenous peoples during the industrialization process under way in the Philippines. The indigenous peoples' movement provided a national and an international context for the Mount Apo story. The symbolic value of the elders' commitment was reflected in the government's efforts to provide "alternative elders" who could rehabilitate the project. Story construction is a particularly important way of communicating performance in situations where public support is a major factor. Of course, public support is often quite important for policy campaign effectiveness, and compelling stories can mobilize that support.

Institutional analysis reminds us that advocacy campaigns take place in wider institutional contexts and may affect those contexts even as they focus on specific policy or practice results. Evidence from analysis of national policy campaigns suggests that policy and practice results may be the tip of a larger and more important iceberg of institutional changes that accompany immediate campaign successes or failures. Campaigns can affect organizations and their members by increasing their capacities for future advocacy or by diverting resources to less productive uses.[6] Campaigns may also create institutional contexts that favor future advocacy activities by, for example, clarifying the contributions of civil society actors, sensitizing targets to the costs of ignoring civil society initiatives, or creating new institutional arrangements that enable more effective advocacy in the future.[7] The institutional impacts of the Mount Apo campaign include strengthening the capacity of the indigenous peoples' movement in the Philippines to influence policy decisions and encouraging the government to be more responsive to such initiatives in the future.

The mix of impact assessment, story construction, and institutional analysis appropriate to the construction of campaign accountability systems will vary with the concerns they seek to address. For all of them, however, data can be collected and interpreted to increase campaign accountability to internal and external stakeholders.

Enabling Performance Consequences

How can campaign accountability systems make information available to stakeholders and enable them to hold the campaign accountable, rewarding good performance and sanctioning bad performance? This is a challenge in most interorganizational domains, and it is complicated by power inequalities and diverse interests across levels in campaign coalitions. Enabling stakeholder sanctions of campaign performance may require different approaches for internal and external stakeholders.

For *internal stakeholders,* campaigns must allocate resources and attention to ensuring that low-power participants, such as grassroots participants, can understand the issues, make their concerns heard, and participate in decisions that affect them. Without explicit attention to such issues, automatic institutional biases favor stakeholders with more capacity to influence targets and more familiarity with policy influence processes. In the Mount Apo campaign, the PDF had better access to the World Bank and the national leadership had better access to the government—so each faced temptations to act on the basis of that information and access alone. The national solidarity councils made listening to the concerns of indigenous elders and other grassroots constituents a priority. Those councils continued throughout the campaign to be wary of the PDF's potential for negotiating deals with the World Bank without consulting indigenous leaders. The relationship between the indigenous leaders and the PDF executive director was critical to the former's trust in her activity and their capacity to hold her accountable.

The problems of power differences can affect accountability to *external stakeholders* as well. Campaigns may have to design ways to become accountable to less powerful stakeholders. Paradoxically, their accountability to the communities they claim to represent can be reinforced by their targets, who may insist on demonstrations of the validity of their claims of accountability to those communities. In the Mount Apo campaign, for example, World Bank missions made a point of checking on the campaign's links to

indigenous groups and came to believe that the campaign did in fact provide good information about indigenous concerns. More generally, the
wider indigenous peoples' movement in the Philippines had real social and
political clout and was positioned to sanction the campaign if it failed to live
up to their expectations. In the politicized context of the campaign, movement leaders outside the campaign could strongly affect public views in
their reactions to government-supported "alternative indigenous leaders"
who spoke in favor of the plant.

In general, explicit attention to arrangements for rewarding or punish-
ing performance is critical when campaigns span a wide range of levels,
interests, and power differences. Without that attention, the campaigns run
the risk of biases that confer too much voice for some stakeholders and too
little for others.

Building Campaign Organization

While existing organizations can easily allocate resources to support
accountability systems, multiorganization campaigns may require substantial investment in new organizational arrangements to articulate
performance expectations, track results, ensure their communication to
stakeholders, and enable performance consequences. In campaign
organizations, organizational arrangements to span power differences as
well as national and regional perspectives are critical to making accountability systems work across the diverse interests among internal and external stakeholders.

The Mount Apo campaign invented the national solidarity councils as
a way of coordinating across local, regional, and national coalition differences. It also delegated responsibility to some members to carry out spe-
cialized elements of the strategy, so the Legal Resources Center handled
litigation in the courts and the PDF provided liaison to the World Bank in
Washington. Other campaigns have developed more elaborate organizational arrangements; for example, the Narmada Action Committee brought
together activists in many different countries to support the campaign
against the Narmada Dams within India.[8] Similarly, the international
alliances of indigenous peoples that emerged from experiences in many
countries gradually built organizations that could enable more effective
coordination and action for indigenous rights in the transnational arena.[9]
Given the autonomy of most campaign members, their accountability
often depends on relationships of mutual trust and shared aspirations
rather than on legal contracts or formal representative mandates. Building
relationships and trust across nations, cultures, and levels plays a critical
role in constructing organizations to support campaign legitimacy and
accountability.

Using Campaign Accountability Systems

Using campaign accountability systems can enhance the capacities and impacts of the campaign itself. That use may also affect discourses in the wider society about campaign issues and the campaign's institutional capacities for dealing with such issues in the future.

Increasing Campaign Capacities

To return to the questions posed by the strategic triangle, the development and use of an accountability system can increase a campaign's ability to create value and expand its operational capacity as well as to enhance its legitimacy and support with key stakeholders.

Information about performance and results can be used for learning purposes, to improve a campaign's *value creation and strategic positioning*. The Mount Apo campaign refocused on indigenous peoples' rights as that issue became more important for both the World Bank and the government of the Philippines. In doing so the campaign positioned itself to build alliances with increasingly strong national and international indigenous peoples' movements. As it became clear that local demonstrations and litigation did not alter government commitment to building the plant, the campaign used that feedback to shift its attention to providing credible information about project problems to potential funders such as the World Bank and other financial institutions.

Accountability system information can also be used to *build operational capacity* for campaign strategies and tactics. Reports from the PDF in Washington enabled the campaign to create credible links to World Bank missions investigating Philippine projects. The success of those links in informing the missions was pivotal to the eventual Bank decision against further support for the Mount Apo project. The national solidarity meetings made it possible for regional and national elements of the campaign to understand and coordinate with local indigenous groups. Without that coordination, government efforts to split the solidarity of local indigenous groups might have been more successful.

The primary rationale for constructing accountability systems is to *strengthen campaign credibility*. Accountability systems can provide direct answers to questions about campaign accountability and indirect support for campaign claims to wider legitimacy. The Mount Apo campaign argued persuasively that it was accountable to local indigenous peoples and so claimed political and performance legitimacy with them and others interested in their welfare. The campaign also argued for normative and regulatory legitimacy in its commitment to implementing national and international policies and values for protecting indigenous rights.

The fact that the campaign alliances and the national solidarity councils included a wide range of concerned groups—farmers, environmentalists, and the Catholic Church as well as indigenous peoples—created associational legitimacy as well. The development of the multileveled campaign and its agreements on accountability expanded its legitimacy with and support from both national and international audiences.

Changing Issue Discourses and Institutions

Transnational campaigns on particular issues can *reshape national discourses and institutions*. Within societies, campaigns that build legitimacy and accountability can raise public awareness of the issues, introduce new arguments into existing discourses, and alter standards, expectation, and institutional contexts in ways that make future campaigns easier. The Mount Apo campaign created wider awareness of the issues of indigenous rights and, more particularly, whether national needs for more power generation capacity could trump those rights in government decisions. Campaigns can sensitize government officials to the possibilities of grassroots resistance or the costs of noncompliance with their own policies. The Philippine energy agency now regrets its failure to develop an acceptable environmental impact assessment for the Mount Apo project; indeed, the government asked for World Bank assistance to increase its capacity for such assessments in the future. Successful campaigns can also alter the constellation of voices heard in national policy making. The Mount Apo campaign built on prior successes of indigenous resistance to large projects, such as the Chico River campaign, to amplify indigenous voices in that decision. The campaign also provided an example for future initiatives by indigenous peoples and others, and it trained a group of activists for effective action in policy campaigns.

Successful campaigns can also alter *international discourses and institutional contexts* as well. The international debate on the rights of indigenous peoples and the institutional role of the World Bank in funding power projects were both influenced by the Mount Apo campaign. While individual Bank projects are difficult to influence once they gain momentum, multiple campaigns against bad projects have reshaped the criteria that control the Bank's project "pipeline" and have established an external audience that monitors and shapes Bank information sharing about future projects and their implementation.[10] The campaign is also highly visible to potential campaigners in other countries as an example of what can be accomplished by determined campaigners. Credible transnational advocacy campaigns raise interests, issues, and problems that might otherwise be ignored; enable the voices of important constituencies; and potentially make important substantive contributions to transnational problem solving and governance.

Summary

This chapter has focused on credibility challenges for transnational advocacy campaigns that bring together organizations across countries and levels. Successful campaign coalitions must deal effectively with power differences among both internal and external stakeholders. As citizens become increasingly aware of the "democracy deficits" that make many existing international institutions insensitive to grassroots interests, transnational advocacy campaigns are likely to become increasingly critical to influencing global public policies and to holding transnational corporations and intergovernmental institutions accountable.[11]

Assessing the legitimacy and accountability of transnational campaigns involves articulating campaign issues and convening members, defining campaign missions and strategies across levels and countries, mapping and prioritizing campaign stakeholders, assessing stakeholder legitimacy and accountability demands, and articulating desired futures for the campaign on these issues. Enhancing campaign legitimacy can focus on demonstrating its fit to existing legitimacy expectations or constructing new standards to fit its goals and activities. Constructing accountability systems requires negotiating expectations with internal and external stakeholders, assessing and communicating campaign performance, enabling performance consequences, and building campaign organization to support continued accountability.

Legitimacy and accountability systems can foster campaign learning that enhances strategic value creation and expands operational capacity as well as strengthening legitimacy and support. Perhaps more important, constructing such systems contribute to a campaign's emergence as a viable national and transnational entity, expanding discourses on the issues and creating an institutional context for wider participation and improved policy making at both national and transnational levels.

Notes

1. I will draw on the analysis of the Mount Apo case in Royo, A., "Against the People's Will: The Mount Apo Story," in *The Struggle for Accountability: NGOs, Social Movements and the World Bank*, ed. J. A. Fox and L. D. Brown (Cambridge, MA: MIT Press, 1998): 151–180. See also Brown, L. D., "Multiparty Social Action and Mutual Accountability," in *Global Accountabilities: Participation, Pluralism and Public Ethics*, ed. Alnoor Ebrahim and Edwin Weisband (Cambridge, UK: Cambridge University Press, 2007): 89–111.

2. See Donnelly, Elizabeth A., "Proclaiming the Jubilee: The Debt and Structural Adjustment Network," in *Restructuring World Politics: Transnational Social Movements, Networks, and Norms*, ed. Sanjeev Khagram,

James V. Riker and Kathryn Sikkink (Minneapolis: University of
Minnesota, 2002): 155–180; Mekata, Motoko, "Building Partnerships
toward a Common Goal: Experiences of the International Campaign to
Ban Landmines," in *The Third Force: The Rise of Transnational Civil Society*,
ed. Ann Florini (Tokyo and Washington: Japan Center for
International Exchange and Carnegie Endowment for International
Peace, 2000): 143–176.

3. Royo, "Against the People's Will" (1998): 163.

4. See analysis of coalitions to influence World Bank projects and
policies in Fox and Brown, *The Struggle for Accountability* (1998), especially
Chapter 12.

5. Miller, Valerie and Razon-Abad, Henedina, "Philippine
Nongovernmental and People's Organizations: What Constitutes
Success in Policy Influence?" in *Policy Influence: NGO Experiences*, ed.
J. Gershman, V. Bourdreau, E. Legaspi, H. Razon-Abad and V. Miller
(Manila: Ateneo Center for Social Policy and Public Affairs, 1997):
172–218.

6. See Miller and Razon-Abad, "Philippine Nongovernment and
People's Organizations" (1997) for discussion of the negative
consequences of campaign participation on NGO institutional development. For a discussion of how campaign capacity building can lead to
future campaigns see also Fox and Brown, *The Struggle for Accountability*
(1998): Chapter 12.

7. See Khagram, Riker and Sikkink, *Restructuring World Politics* (2001);
and Risse, T., "The Power of Norms vs. the Norms of Power:
Transnational Civil Society and Human Rights," in *The Third Force*
(2001): 177–210. See also Udall, L., "The World Bank and Public
Accountability: Has Anything Changed?" in *The Struggle for Accountability*
(1998): 391–436 for a discussion of institutional changes that have
enabled more advocacy on Bank Projects.

8. Udall, "The World Bank and Public Accountability" (1998).

9. Gray, Andrew, "Development Policy—Development Protest: The
World Bank, Indigenous Peoples, and NGOs," in *The Struggle for
Accountability* (1998): 267–302.

10. See Udall, "The World Bank and Public Accountability" (1998);
and Fox, J. A., and Brown, L. D., "Assessing the Impacts of NGO
Advocacy Campaigns on World Bank Projects and Policies," in *The
Struggle for Accountability* (1998): 495–551.

11. See Clark, John, *Worlds Apart: Civil Society and the Battle for Ethical
Globalization* (Bloomfield, CT: Kumarian Press, 2003); and Reinicke,
Wolfgang and Deng, Francis, *Critical Choices: The United Nations, Networks
and the Future of Global Governance* (Ottawa: International Development
Research Centre, 2000).

CHAPTER EIGHT

Negotiating Cross-Sector Partnership Credibility

In the late 1990s, reports from two small NGOs, Global Witness and Partnership Africa Canada, documented how the failure to regulate trade in African "conflict diamonds" fueled ongoing rebellions and civilian atrocities in Angola, the Democratic Republic of Congo, and Sierra Leone. Over the next three years, diamond companies, NGOs, governments, and UN agencies met in a series of frequently stormy meetings known as the Kimberly Process and negotiated agreement on a process to regulate trade in illicit diamonds.[1] By 2006 more than seventy countries had signed the agreement, which was supported by major diamond companies, the UN, and a broad coalition of international NGOs. Enforcement of the agreement reduced the conflict diamond share of the world diamond trade from as much as 15 percent in the late 1990s to less than 1 percent in 2006.[2]

The Kimberly Process is an example of the creation of a *cross-sector partnership* that includes parties from different institutional sectors such as government agencies, businesses, and civil society organizations (CSOs). Transnational cross-sector partnerships bring together organizations across national and regional boundaries as well as across sectoral differences. Sector associations bring together organizations involved in similar activities, and campaign coalitions bring together actors from different levels and perspectives committed to campaign goals. Transnational cross-sector partnerships, in contrast, involve actors from different sectors, different countries, and different levels who have stakes in the management of some transnational issue or problem.

Negotiating credibility for cross-sector partnerships involves dealing with diverse assumptions about goals, interests, and roles. It is not uncommon, for example, for different sectors to question each other's legitimacy as actors on the problem. Often representatives of different sectors see each other as primary contributors to problems. Civil society actors may blame corporate greed and government corruption, business leaders may blame government corruption and civil society ideologies, and governments may blame corporate greed and civil society ideologies. While some cross-sector initiatives start from the altruism of one or more parties, it is probably more common for them to start from positions of skepticism or outright conflict over appropriate solutions.[3]

Cross-sector partnerships are also often characterized by differences in wealth and power among the actors. Many transnational corporations or intergovernmental organizations such as the World Bank have resources far beyond those of the civil society organizations who seek to influence transnational problem solving. Many civil society campaign coalitions struggle to mobilize the information, finances, and public visibility that can balance the resources of national governments, intergovernmental organizations, and transnational corporations.

This chapter focuses on the special challenges of negotiating legitimacy and accountability expectations in transnational cross-sector partnerships. Such partnerships are frequently created to deal with international issues that are beyond the problem-solving capacities of any sector acting alone. Thus in recent years we have seen cross-sector problem-solving initiatives to regulate transnational marketing practices,[4] control and reform corrupt practices in transnational development,[5] regulate large dam construction,[6] foster intersectoral social learning on critical issues,[7] and act on a variety of other transnational public issues.[8] More generally, future global problem solving is expected to require more extensive use of cross-sector deliberation and collective action to respond rapidly and effectively to emerging problems that threaten to overwhelm the capacities of existing transnational institutions.[9]

As in prior chapters, this one will examine four aspects of legitimacy and accountability of cross-sector partnerships: (1) assessing their legitimacy and accountability challenges, (2) enhancing partnership internal and external legitimacy, (3) constructing accountability systems to deal with claims of partnership stakeholders, and (4) using legitimacy and accountability resources to advance the partnership's mission. The cross-sector partnership of the Kimberly Process, established to regulate the trade in rough diamonds, will be used to illustrate the challenges and possibilities of enhancing the credibility of such partnerships.[10]

Assessing Cross-Sector Partnership Legitimacy and Accountability

Cross-sector partnerships bring together actors from two or more sectors to work on problems whose solutions often require the information and capacities of more than one sector. Research indicates that cross-sector partnerships have been especially common in turbulent environments where old solutions are no longer appropriate; they can address problems for which single-sector solutions have been inadequate.[11] The role of diamonds in generating endless conflict and atrocities in Africa was long obscured by lack of information and political turbulence in the region. However, once it became clear that the trade in illicit diamonds financed continuing rebellions by gangsters who had control of alluvial diamond fields but no public support, it also became clear that a transnational cross-sector partnership would be necessary to regulate the diamond trade.

Recognition that a problem requires cross-sector cooperation is not automatic. The cross-sector engagement required to create a partnership that can hold its members accountable does not occur without willingness by some partners to invest in creating cooperation. Assessing the legitimacy and accountability challenges of a cross-sector partnership involves five elements: (1) articulating issues and convening potential partners, (2) defining partnership missions and strategies, (3) mapping the partnership's internal and external stakeholders, (4) assessing its legitimacy and accountability demands and priorities, and (5) articulating visions for a desired partnership future.

Articulating Issues and Convening Potential Partners

Many emerging transnational problems too easily "fall between the cracks" left by existing institutional arrangements. Often those institutions were created to deal with different problems, or they are too weak to take effective action. For many problems the costs are born by powerless and voiceless populations, while gains from the status quo accrue to relatively powerful constituencies. Sometimes the positive products of the problems are much more visible than their negative consequences, or the causal links that create positive and negative consequences of a situation have not been made explicit. Often parties generate competing explanations that blame each other for the problem.

Building a cross-sector partnership requires a problem definition that can be accepted across sectors and can also provide a base on which to construct solutions. Articulating the issues for cross-sector collaboration also requires identifying incentives that are compelling for diverse parties: civil society organizations, for example, may be motivated by concerns of marginalized populations, whereas governments have to consider political constituencies, and corporations remain responsible to their owners. It is also critical to identify how different partners can contribute to problem solving, as it is seldom obvious why the parties should tolerate the tensions of joint action. Finally, convening the right partners may be challenging, particularly if there is a history of conflict or distrust among key parties.

The issue of conflict diamonds and their role in human rights atrocities in several African countries remained "beneath the radar" of governments and corporations involved in the diamond trade for many years. In 1998 a report from Global Witness documented the role of illicit diamonds in supporting the UNITA rebellion in Angola that killed hundreds of thousands of Angolans in spite of having little or no popular support. UNITA was able to continue because of its control of most of Angola's diamonds. A year later, Partnership Africa Canada released a similar analysis of the Revolutionary United Front in Sierra Leone, which made a practice of amputating hands and feet of civilians to frighten them out of the diamond fields and used its control of those fields to purchase weapons. The two NGOs raised an issue that had remained publicly unrecognized by either the diamond industry or the governments involved—and the consequences of the illicit diamond trade began to receive significant public attention. A UN Security Council study confirmed the link between diamonds and weapons, and a UN report for the first time named heads of state as accomplices in violating UN sanctions by trafficking in diamonds and guns.

The combination of these reports got serious attention from the diamond industry. De Beers, the company that has historically controlled more than half of the world's rough diamond trade, closed its offices for buying diamonds from outside its own mines. Many corporations were acutely aware of the diamond market's vulnerability to publicity about "blood diamonds." The government of South Africa, also sensitive to the danger of diamond boycotts, convened the first meeting of the Kimberly Process in 2000. That meeting brought together interested governments, NGOs, and representatives of the diamond industry, so for the first time many key actors from different sectors could deal with each other face to face. At that first meeting, the group made no decisions, but it did agree to meet again. In a dozen meetings over the next three years—meetings often characterized by disagreements and shouting matches—the participants ultimately agreed on the importance of preventing trade in diamonds that would support further conflicts.

Defining Cross-Sector Partnership Mission and Strategy

It may be quite difficult to construct overarching goals and strategies that are meaningful to all the parties. Negotiating compromises or dovetailing diverse interests may be central to creating partnerships. While diamond-trading corporations and country governments can agree that it is important to sustain and further develop the diamond trade, CSOs and local populations might see local security and benefits as much more important. Working out an agreement that produces both outcomes may be central to the partnership's credibility as a response to the conflict diamonds problem.

The challenge of building a mission and a strategy for a cross-sector partnership can be complicated by histories of mistrust, conflict, and blame. It has often been difficult to develop shared missions and strategies unless the failure of sectors acting alone becomes obvious to all. The World Commission on Dams, for example, emerged from years of struggle between governments, intergovernmental organizations, transnational corporations, international NGOs, and grassroots movements with stakes in dam construction that produced stalemates in many different countries. Creating a cross-sector commission charged with evaluating past dam performance and articulating standards for future dam construction was an effort to solve problems with building large dams that had not been solved by the parties acting independently.[12]

The strategic triangle can be applied to understanding the challenges facing cross-sector partnerships. Figure 8.1 presents the diverse partners that must agree about partnership mission and strategy. Positioning member strategic triangles so their value-creation apexes come together at a center point reflects the need for agreement on value creation in spite of their diverse operational capacities and legitimacy and support contexts. The development of partnership operating capacity, support, and legitimacy

Figure 8.1 Cross-Sector Partnership Strategic Triangle

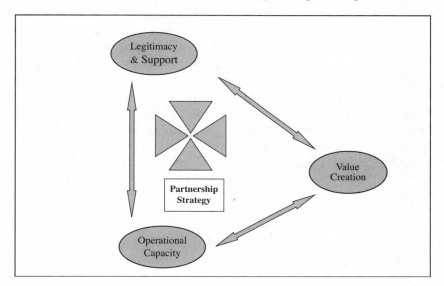

often follows agreement on the need for joint value creation. The creation of a shared strategy and mission within a cross-sector partnership often requires considerable negotiation about goals, interests, and perceptions of the problem.

Missions and strategies often include a diagnosis of the problems they seek to solve, some articulation of a future desired state, and a theory of change that describes how to move from the present problem to the desired state. In the Kimberly Process, for example, it was clear to some participants before the first meeting that the problem of conflict diamonds presented a significant threat to the global diamond trade and the governments and corporations that benefit from it. The example of the civil society campaigns that produced boycotts and long-term decline of the fur trade was very salient to De Beers and the government of South Africa when they convened the first meeting in Kimberly.

The importance of creating a cross-sector partnership was less clear to others. It required a dozen meetings and three years to build credibility with other governments, corporations, and CSOs. Eventually more than seventy governments and many corporations agreed to participate, and CSOs including Amnesty International, Oxfam International, World Vision, and several African networks joined the NGOs that first raised the issue. The Kimberly Process also built the operational capacity required to implement the proposed regulations.

Cross-sector partnerships must grapple with the reality that its members face different authorizing contexts and use different criteria for assessing value creation. Much of the challenge of building shared partnership strategy is in aligning these contexts and criteria to support joint action. Corporate partners must account to their shareholders for how participation will contribute to long-term profitability, government partners must explain to their constituents why participation contributes to citizen welfare, and civil society actors must be able to show members and donors why their involvement advances their missions. The potential for permanent harm to the market for diamonds was raised frequently by corporate and government partners in the Kimberly Process as a rationale for their involvement, in part because they recognized that the upsurge in public visibility of conflict diamonds and their consequences, highlighted by journalists and filmmakers, could prepare the way for a devastating consumer backlash.

Mapping Cross-Sector Stakeholders

The stakeholders in cross-sectoral partnerships are often even more diverse than the stakeholders in campaigns or sectors, since they come from different sectors and bring very different goals, interests, and perspectives to

Figure 8.2 Kimberly Process Stakeholders

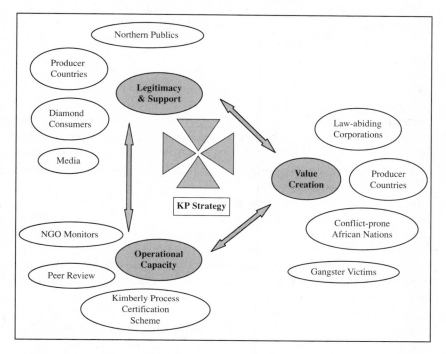

the table. As in other domains, it is important to assess both internal stakeholders that are members of the partnership and external stakeholders that affect or are affected by its activities.

Figure 8.2 provides an overview of stakeholders who are important in the Kimberly Process for regulating conflict diamonds. The primary internal constituents include corporations in the diamond industry, governments concerned with regulating that industry, intergovernmental organizations interested in peacekeeping and development, and NGOs involved in campaigning to regulate the trade. Over the course of the Kimberly Process, an increasing number of governments with stakes in the diamond trade became involved, including the diamond markets of the Netherlands and the US, the diamond-cutting industry in Belgium, India, and Israel, and the producer countries of South Africa, Namibia, Canada, Botswana, and Russia. The diamond industry involved De Beers and other major firms as well as the World Diamond Council, an association created by the diamond industry after the first conflict diamond stories broke. The NGOs that initially raised the issue were reinforced by

CSOs with capacity for mobilizing widespread public pressure, such as Amnesty International, Oxfam International, and World Vision.

The Kimberly Process also had a wide range of external stakeholders, some of whom—such as the populations subject to rebellions and terrorism in producer countries—had large stakes and little voice in the Process. What might have been insuperable differences in wealth and power were to some extent balanced by the growing media interest in the issue and its potential for influencing future consumers. In effect this public interest tended to level the playing field and increase government and industry concern about legitimacy and support for the trade. A key factor in the Process was the gradual development of an enforceable regulatory system that could sanction noncompliance by corporations and governments. For the Kimberly Process, as for many other transnational problem domains, the problem is exacerbated by the fact that some powerful parties, such as the diamond trading companies, make concentrated gains from the status quo while many others, such as populations oppressed by "revolutionary" gangs, carry costs that are largely invisible to transnational decision makers.

An important aspect of stakeholder mapping in cross-sector partnerships is recognizing impacts on populations that might otherwise be ignored. Part of the reason that the conflict diamond problem persisted and grew was because it was invisible to many stakeholders. The ultimate customers of the diamond trade, for example, did not recognize the high prices being paid by the populations of diamond-producing countries to make "cheap" diamonds available. When Global Witness and Partnership Africa Canada published their analyses, they made those hidden costs more widely visible. They demonstrated that previously unrecognized stakeholders were suffering grievous harm from the trade in illicit diamonds.

The revelation of these consequences changed the stakeholder map for the trade. In revealing the fate of "invisible stakeholders," the CSOs made possible publicity, boycotts, and other interventions that would severely harm the industry's long-term prospects. This revelation got the attention of corporations, such as De Beers, and governments, such as the government of South Africa, whose well-being was closely tied to the health of the industry, and so altered the audibility of the voices of previously unheard stakeholders.

Assessing Cross-Sector Legitimacy and Accountability Demands

The challenges of building legitimacy and accountability for transnational cross-sector problem solving may be particularly difficult when differences in perspective and interest across sectors and levels are extreme.

The concerns of major diamond traders in Antwerp and New York are very far from the concerns of subsistence farmers living in alluvial diamond regions in Sierra Leone or Angola or the concerns of the governments of those countries. Assessing the legitimacy of cross-sector partnerships focuses attention on their roles as transnational actors whose activities reverberate across sectors.

The most important *bases for the legitimacy* of cross-sector partnerships in transnational contexts often include performance and normative elements. Partnerships are usually expected to deliver concrete performance benefits that justify their costs, and they may also construct accounts for their activities that reflect values and norms held across the countries, sectors, and levels. Those benefits may be differently defined by different stakeholders. Government and company partners to the Kimberly Process hoped to preserve and expand the diamond trade, the NGOs hoped to reduce human rights violations, and other governments and intergovernmental agencies hoped to reduce endless internal conflicts. In some cases cross-sector partnerships gain legitimacy from enabling voice to marginalized populations, though formal political bases for legitimacy are less common than performance and normative bases. Associational bases of legitimacy may be less important, given the diverse priorities and associations of the partners, but in some cases the partnership may gain legitimacy with some external stakeholders because of its linkage to diverse participants. Regulatory legitimacy based on compliance with laws may be a product of the partnership, as in the Kimberly Process, but lack of common regulations across national and sectoral boundaries are often part of the initial problem, and cognitive legitimacy is typically less potent in circumstances where understanding of problems and their effects is just emerging.

The challenges to cross-sector partnerships are often framed in performance terms. Partners or external stakeholders whose interests are potentially or actually undermined by the partnership's activities can be expected to raise questions. Others may question the extent to which partnership goals are in fact being achieved by the partnership's expenditures. The Kimberly Process, for example, has been criticized by countries whose trade in diamonds has been reduced by its regulations. More importantly, a three-year evaluation of the program's performance criticized its failure to regulate some countries and its inadequate resources for implementation. Assessing legitimacy involves identifying existing and potential challenges whose resolution would enhance future legitimacy claims.

Assessing partnership accountabilities focuses on more specific performance expectations of the partnership and its members, particularly expectations that strengthen or weaken its legitimacy in the wider transnational context. Transnational cross-sector partnerships, similar to sector alliances and campaign coalitions, can develop shared goals, strong relationships, and mutual accountability systems that allow mutual influence. However, the initial differences of interest and perspective across sectors, levels, and countries can make building mutual accountability very difficult and time consuming. The construction of the Kimberly Process required three years of meetings and considerable conflict before the parties agreed on processes and systems for regulating the diamond trade. Given the stakes involved and the need for explicit enforcement, the systems for regulating trade in diamonds could not have been implemented without formal mechanisms and contractual accountability systems.

Assessing partnership accountability demands will turn on the nature of the problem to be solved; the resources, capacities, and willingness of the partners; and the relationships among them that can support joint action. In the Kimberly Process, for example, assessing national performance was essential to creating an effective system—but governments were very reluctant to commit to a mandatory inspection process. After much discussion they agreed to "voluntary inspections." In practice most governments eventually agreed to participate in inspections rigorous enough to result in sanctions, so the informal process eventually created regulations that could be used to hold members accountable for violations and eject violators from the partnership. As the Kimberly Process illustrates, accountability demands can be expected to vary over the life of a partnership, evolving as systems are developed and problems are encountered.

Articulating Visions for the Future

How can enhancing the legitimacy and accountability of cross-sector partnerships help accomplish their missions? The creation and maintenance of partnerships across sectors is difficult and expensive in time, energy, and resources. What expected outcomes and desired future states can justify that investment?

Part of the challenge of articulating desired future states is the need to frame the present state as problematic. Cross-sector partnerships in the past have often emerged from histories of "sector failure," situations in which actors from one sector have been unable to deal with a problem but cross-sector cooperation has offered possible solutions. The World Commission on Dams, for example, grew out of decades of inconclusive and mutually costly struggle among governments, intergovernmental organizations, social movements, NGOs, and others over the construction of large dams. In other cases, some new analysis has revealed underlying causes that require cross-sector action. The causal links among human rights atrocities, interminable "rebellions," and illicit trade in conflict diamonds remained largely invisible until the NGO studies demonstrated the connections. When those links were revealed and combined with the possibility of a global consumer boycott of diamonds, the issue became a serious problem for many actors who had previously been comfortably unaware of it.

Compelling visions for cross-sector partnerships have to take into account the diverse interests and incentives of different sectors. Constructing such visions may call for creative synthesis and dovetailing of interests and incentives into visions that are attractive to diverse parties. "Success" for the Kimberly Process might mean preservation and expansion of the market for the diamond industry, economic growth and reduced intrastate conflict for governments and intergovernmental agencies, and reduction in human rights violations and local atrocities for NGOs. While it is often easy to gain agreement on general principles for such visions, the details of implementation often generate controversy and further negotiation. But without the general statement of partnership aspirations, it is almost impossible to negotiate agreement on implementation details.

Enhancing Partnership Legitimacy

Enhancing the legitimacy of cross-sector partnerships may involve special resources and challenges. The establishment of a cross-sector partnership may confer some legitimacy on its activities by its very existence. The fact that leaders from different sectors are participating may enhance the partnership's legitimacy with those sectors by association. On the other hand, the fact that cross-sector partnerships have roots in different sectors also means that they have to meet different standards and expectations to appear legitimate across such different contexts. The Kimberly Process ultimately is legitimate if it lives up to many different goals and standards.

Demonstrating Fit with Existing Standards

Many approaches to enhancing legitimacy involve demonstrating the fit between the partnership's activities and impacts and existing legitimacy expectations. Partnerships can conform to existing legitimacy expectations or inform stakeholders about how they are meeting those expectations. When cross-sector partnerships are innovations for which few expectations exist, their legitimacy may turn on meeting existing expectations for their members, such as market, state, and civil society legitimacy criteria. But meeting all those standards and expectations may be very difficult, even when the participation of key actors from different sectors provides some legitimacy by association from the start.

The legitimacy of the Kimberly Process depended early on its potential for simultaneously serving the interests and goals of the diamond industry, national governments, and NGOs concerned with development and human rights. Attention was given to informing constituents about how the partnership would advance the interests of their members as well as wider publics and African populations affected by the illicit diamond trade. Partnerships may also enhance their legitimacy through association with credible actors. In some cases approval or support from actors with high credibility may be critical. Strong support for the Kimberly Process from the government of South Africa and the De Beers company was central to its early success in attracting key actors to the negotiations.

Constructing New Partnership Standards

In problem arenas where cross-sector partnerships amount to an institutional innovation, enhancing legitimacy may require constructing new standards and expectations. Where cross-sector partnerships are already accepted as a standard approach to solving social problems, it may be easier to launch them. But for the challenge of regulating the trade in conflict diamonds, many key actors had little experience with cross-sector collaboration. They were inclined to see each other as part of the problem, so joint action was not an immediately obvious option. In the medium term, performance and normative legitimacy could be achieved by demonstrating the partnership's capacity to regulate the trade in illicit diamonds and their impact on funding rebellions. In the short term, however, the partnership needed the resources of governments and industry for pragmatic legitimacy, the support of constituents of governments and civil society for political legitimacy, and the value of principled behavior and knowledge by all the parties to create normative legitimacy. Over time, the Kimberly Process used these resources to build a legitimacy base that eventually made it possible to recruit seventy governments as signatories.

Building legitimacy with external stakeholders depended on demonstrating that the Kimberly Process could regulate the diamond trade and that signatories would be accountable for enforcing agreements. As described above, many governments initially rejected a mandatory inspection process that would unveil violations, so the agreement provided for a "voluntary" inspection process rather than a mandatory enforcement system. Over the first few years, however, the "voluntary" process was accepted by so many members that it became normatively expected. Indeed, the Process then ejected from membership countries such as Congo (Brazzaville) that did not measure up to its evolving standards. So while the initial accountability model of the Process was a weak form of mutual accountability, engagement over time strengthened that accountability and enhanced the overall legitimacy of the partnership. In problems areas where the stakes for violating agreements are high, the legitimacy of the partnership may depend very directly on clear and effective systems for holding key actors accountable for living up to expectations.

Constructing Cross-Sector Accountability Systems

The assessment of accountability for partnerships provides the base for constructing cross-sector accountability systems. That construction involves (1) negotiating cross-sector stakeholder expectations, (2) assessing and communicating performance, (3) enabling performance consequences, and (4) building cross-sector organizations that can implement accountability systems across national, sectoral, and level differences.

Negotiating Stakeholder Expectations

Cross-sector partnerships pose questions about accountability among the partners, such as the actors in the Kimberly Process, and between the partnership and its external stakeholders. Initial negotiations focus on actual and potential partners. These negotiations can be conflict-prone, particularly when the parties have histories of disagreement and bring very different interests to the table. Initial meetings of the Kimberly Process, for example, were characterized by conflicts and "shouting matches." While most parties agreed that the diamond trade should not support gangsters and atrocities, there was little agreement on how to accomplish their aspirations.

Successful negotiations among internal stakeholders create agreements on the problems, the desired results of the partnership, and the ways in which the parties will contribute to reaching those results. They help define the identity and goals of a successful partnership. They also suggest the responsibilities of the partners and the outcomes associated with living up to those responsibilities—in other words, the dimensions of internal stakeholder accountability.

Relations with external stakeholders often reflect the goals and expectations of partners to the initiative, and those relations may also affect how members deal with each other. During establishment of the Kimberly Process, partners from different sectors were concerned about different aspects of the illicit diamond trade. Industry representatives wanted to avoid consumer boycotts and reassure potential customers. Government representatives hoped to preserve the diamond trade and reduce endless violent rebellions. NGOs were concerned about atrocities by armed groups in control of diamond fields. Many partners were concerned about the role of the media: high-visibility television and movie treatments and celebrity involvement with conflict diamonds created urgent concern with wider publics. The threat of unfavorable publicity helped balance the power inequalities among governments, businesses, and NGOs. In this way, accountabilities among partners were reinforced by the interest of external stakeholders—customers, UN agencies, and general publics—in better regulation of conflict diamonds.

Assessing Partnership Results

The diverse agendas and interests of the cross-sector partners put a premium on concrete results that would be meaningful across diverse perspectives. Four kinds of indicators are commonly treated as evidence of success in cross-sector problem solving: evidence that the initial problem has been solved or reduced, indications that the circumstances of partners have improved, data that relationships have been enhanced, and evidence of positive indirect effects from the partnership.

Indicators of *improvement in the initial problem* depend on the nature of that problem. The World Commission on Dams, for example, was charged with assessing the performance of large dams and creating standards for their construction in the future that could be accepted by a wide range of stakeholders.[13] Indicators of success in that partnership would be wide acceptance of their assessments and standards by diverse partners—a result partially but not completely achieved by the Commission's deliberations and report. For the Kimberly Process, regulation of the illicit trade in conflict diamonds required that many countries accept and enforce new processes and standards to export and import rough diamonds. While the initial standards and procedures were less rigorous than some partners wanted, the Process appears to have improved its capacities to regulate the trade over the first three years. Problem-related indicators include immediate outputs of the Process, outcomes in terms of changed behavior by key actors, and longer-term impacts such as reductions in illicit diamond trade. While it is difficult to create measures of impacts that are causally distant from partnership activities, tools for constructing logical frameworks and persuasive change theories have been multiplying over the last decade.[14]

Success may also be defined in terms of *impacts on particular stakeholders*. For many partners, participation in the partnership must be justified by results consistent with their missions. For the Kimberly Process, some corporate and government partners equated success with a viable and growing trade in rough diamonds. Civil society partners expected success to reduce the capacity of armed groups to continue "wars of liberation" financed by diamonds rather than by popular support. Some African governments also hoped that trade regulation would reduce costly internal conflicts financed with illicit diamonds. Different stakeholders had quite different definitions of what results would indicate success from their particular perspectives.

A third set of partnership indicators emphasizes *improved relationships among partners*. The parties to the Kimberly Process had little contact with each other prior to the crisis posed by the conflict diamonds problem. Over the course of a dozen meetings, increased understanding, respect, and mutual influence were built among participating corporate, government, intergovernmental, and civil society organizations. In many transnational and intersectoral problems, the development of social capital among key stakeholders is critical to effective joint action.[15] That capital can be reused in future problem solving, so it is an independently valuable product of successful cross-sector cooperation across transnational boundaries.[16]

Finally, cross-sector partnerships may create *indirect impacts that benefit wider constituencies*. Successful partnerships may create innovations that can be applied to many other problems. The World Commission on Dams offers a model for cross-sector learning that can be applied to other similar issues such as problems of infrastructure development, water distribution, or environmental conservation. Partnerships may also have impacts that are indirect consequences of problem solving. The regulation of the diamond trade by the Kimberly Process is expected to reduce the incentives for conflict and atrocities financed by illicit diamonds in several countries, and potentially to contribute to peace and development initiatives. Cross-sector models can be adapted to many different situations, including a wide range of transnational problems that are now not handled well by existing institutional arrangements.[17]

Combinations of performance measures can be used to assess outputs, outcomes, and impacts on partnership problems, internal stakeholders, stakeholder relationships, and indirect results. The value of indicators must also be balanced against the costs of collecting and analyzing them. In transnational cross-sectoral initiatives, monitoring performance and interpreting results can be challenging. Data are difficult to acquire and may not be available for long periods. Interpreting impacts is always subject to misattribution or ambiguity, particularly when many actors contribute to them. Part of the problem for the Kimberly Process is a long chain of activities that begins in the African bush, where events are not easily monitored, and culminates in affluent shops on other continents. Major elements of the Kimberly Process focused on developing ways to monitor each link in that long chain so that results could not be easily manipulated.

Enabling Cross-Sector Performance Consequences

Cross-sector accountability requires that stakeholders reward good performance and sanction bad performance. The partnership's reputation and identity depend on its ability to create performance consequences for its members.[18] The partnership can enhance its legitimacy by clear accountability to complaints from both internal and external stakeholders that are affected by or affect its operations. Enabling performance consequences requires a communication system to make performance information available, and it requires stakeholder access to rewards and punishments to address that performance.

Communication systems that make performance data available can be problematic in transnational cross-sector initiatives that include stakeholders at multiple levels, with diverse interests and skills, operating in different languages, and concerned about different interests and indicators. While negotiating stakeholder expectations can build agreement about performance expectations, subsistence farmers in rural Angola and diamond buyers in New York City pose very different communication challenges. Different stakeholders want different data and responding to many claims can be very expensive, so partnership leaders must focus on communicating important information in terms appropriate to critical stakeholders.

Problems of power inequalities surface early in cross-sector partnerships, and genuine partnerships create some degree of mutual accountability to make use of different partners' resources. But mobilizing performance sanctions, especially by low-power stakeholders, can still present thorny problems. Partners are understandably reluctant to accept sanctions for poor performance—but they risk their legitimacy with wider publics if they ignore feedback and sanctions from key stakeholders. In the Kimberly Process, for example, governments and industry initially blocked civil society proposals for formal independent evaluations of country compliance and instead adopted "informal peer evaluations." It became a norm among signatories, however, to request those peer evaluations, and failure to meet peer standards resulted in the expulsion of Congo (Brazzaville). The partnership also agreed to systematic evaluation by NGO members and responded positively to a strong critique after the first three years. For partnerships that are highly visible to wider publics, public challenges can produce real sanctions.

Efforts to build sanctions that create performance consequences are increasingly central to creating cross-sector partnerships with legitimacy as problem-solving initiatives. The UN's Global Compact has been criticized for emphasizing "learning" rather than "enforcing" business innovations that support human rights, environment, and labor standards. The World Bank's Inspection Panel has created a vehicle by which low-power stakeholders can question Bank projects, and the Human Accountability Project International has created a vehicle for vulnerable populations to hold humanitarian assistance and relief NGOs accountable. Many initiatives are exploring how to assess cross-sector partnerships and enable multistakeholder assessment and feedback.[19]

Building Cross-Sector Organizations

Implementing transnational cross-sector initiatives often requires organizational arrangements that bridge the differences among the partners and coordinate problem solving. Even for short-term initiatives, effective action across such differences may require special organizational arrangements. For example, the World Commission on Dams needed a strong secretariat to carry out research, support the commissioners, and maintain links to external constituents to carry out the Commission's mandate over a two-year period. Building an effective cross-sector organization is even more important for problems that have no time limit and require continued monitoring and enforcement, such as the regulation of the diamond trade.

At least three challenges confront transnational cross-sector organizations: bridging differences among members and external stakeholders, carrying out tasks required to achieve their mission and goals, and adapting to experience and changing circumstances. *Bridging differences* to establish communication, trust, and mutual accountability is essential to launching cross-sector initiatives. Three years of meetings of the Kimberly Process gradually constructed bridges among the executives of diamond corporations, representatives of interested governments, NGO delegates, and others, enabling them to hammer out agreements—often via vigorous arguments and denunciations—about how they could together regulate the diamond trade. These relationships were the basis for defining and accepting the Kimberly Process Certification Scheme (KPCS) as an organizational vehicle for regulating diamond imports and exports.

Cross-sector organizations often *carry out very diverse tasks* to achieve their missions and goals. The World Commission on Dams produced research on dam performance and articulated principles for creating new dams, so it supplemented its secretariat with consultants and advisory bodies that did research and organized engagements with diverse constituencies. Regulating the trade in rough diamonds required that the KPCS develop a certification process to prevent trade in illicit diamonds. The KPCS organization, eventually joined by more than seventy countries, regulates the import and export of rough diamonds by issuing a certificate for each exported diamond, ensuring that it is "conflict-free" because it can be tracked back to where it was mined. Signatories agree to block imports of rough diamonds without a KPCS certificate. The system also produces statistics that can be compared across countries to make sure it is working. Working groups composed of government, industry and civil society representatives handle the statistics, monitoring, technical issues, and membership. A peer review mechanism reviews country performance to ensure they meet standards. This review process has sometimes terminated country memberships in the KPCS and so has established credibility as more than a cosmetic process. Partnership tasks may be long-term, technical, and difficult, requiring significant organization and investment.

Short-term cross-sector initiatives may not survive long enough to require review and revision in the light of experience or changing external circumstances. Longer-term initiatives, however, must adapt to change, particularly as they expand operations or as new challenges emerge. The KPCS carried out a third-year review in 2006. At a plenary meeting in Botswana, an NGO delegate noted:

> We meet at a moment of great importance for the Kimberly Process. . . . In the past 18 months, we have seen more and more examples of how criminals and diamond dealers and smugglers and even governments have been able to bypass, subvert and ignore the KPCS with almost complete impunity.[20]

With support from the chairman of the World Diamond Council, the meeting dealt with immediate problems of smuggling and government resistance to regulation and accepted all forty-three recommendations of the review, including controversial matters such as increasing statistical transparency, assessing penalties for noncompliance, and enhancing KPCS financial viability. These changes revived the optimism of many participants about the long-term effectiveness of the KPCS. But, as in the initial construction of the Process, revision to adapt to changing challenges was another occasion for managing cross-sector differences in perception and interests among the partners.

Using Cross-Sector Accountability Systems

Accountability systems for cross-sector partnerships, like those for sector associations or advocacy campaigns, can be used to accomplish multiple purposes beyond their primary goal of enhancing credibility.

Strengthening Problem Solving

Cross-sector partnerships have great promise for solving complex problems that require the resources of different sectors and countries. Cross-sector accountability systems enable partners to hold each other accountable and external stakeholders to hold the partnership accountable. They may also be used to enhance strategic value creation and operational capacity as well as increasing the legitimacy of the partnership.

A cross-sector accountability system can *strengthen the legitimacy* of the partnership as a governance or problem-solving mechanism. It can clarify stakeholder expectations for partnership performance, provide information about how expectations are being met, and offer remedies when expectations are unfulfilled. It can answer questions about "accountable to whom, and for what and how?" and contribute to answering questions of partnership legitimacy as a transnational institution. The review of the KPCS raised questions about member performance, and its actions on those questions strengthened its internal and external legitimacy. Such reviews can strengthen the legitimacy of negotiated cross-sector regulatory processes in the transnational arena, where regulation by global authorities is notoriously difficult.

Using a cross-sector accountability system can also *build operational capacity* for transnational problem solving and governance. Capacity building is often critical to handling transnational problems, particularly when institutional innovation is necessary. Information produced by the KPCS revealed that some countries were not complying with system standards; reviews emphasized those failures and proposed capacity building to remedy them. Combining the resources of different sectors can catalyze innovative solutions to capacity problems. The KPCS made extensive use of volunteer services from its members to develop and implement the Process, and its members also eventually responded to the need for financial investment to professionalize and expand it. Information from accountability systems can catalyze capacity building to deal with performance problems or with shifting contextual demands.

Using accountability systems can also enhance the capacity of cross-sectoral initiatives to engage in *strategic learning about value creation*. Unvarnished feedback from reviews enabled KPCS to recognize important crossroads in its evolution and to confront violations of its standards, invest in enhanced capacity, and build stronger institutional bases for its regulatory work. Without that feedback, the intersectoral bickering that had paralyzed institutional strengthening in the prior eighteen months would have continued, to the long-term detriment of the partnership and its purpose.[21]

Building Transnational Regimes

Chapter 2 suggested that civil society legitimacy and accountability are particularly problematic in transnational contexts because of limited institutions for transnational governance, poorly understood transnational problems, and the challenges of organizing civil society actors across national boundaries. Cross-sector initiatives have demonstrated substantial potential for constructing transnational regimes that have large impacts on international problems. In particular, cross-sector initiatives have shaped public awareness of previously unrecognized problems, catalyzed debates and evolving discourses on appropriate responses, and helped create institutions for identifying and solving transnational problems.

The creation of cross-sector accountability systems often involves widespread *recognition of a problem,* often a problem that has not been visible before. The recognition that free samples of infant formula mixed with unsafe water in developing countries often caused infant deaths from diarrhea led to a widespread campaign—and ultimately a cross-sector partnership—to regulate corporate marketing practices in the developing world.[22] The cross-sector initiative to regulate trade in rough diamonds grew out of civil society and UN exposés of their use to finance armed rebellions and atrocities in Africa. Public revulsion for the practices of diamond-financed warlords fueled the creation of the KPCS to regulate the trade. Cross-sector initiatives can build widespread recognition of the links between transnational processes and actors in events that were previously not visible or understood.

A second consequence of cross-sector problem analyses can be the creation of *consensus on desired future states.* The upshot of debates over the infant formula controversy was a widespread agreement that marketing practices should not increase the risk of babies dying. The debates over conflict diamonds established that the general public does not want the diamond trade to encourage the amputation of the limbs of African children. While not all cross-sector partnerships are grounded in such flammable issues, it is common for civil society actors to mobilize cross-sector initiatives around widely held values. Public discourses about values can encourage government and corporate participation that might otherwise be unlikely. The participation of De Beers and the South African government in the Kimberly Process was grounded in part on the recognition that the diamond trade might be seriously harmed by values-driven consumer boycotts.

Cross-sector initiatives in the transnational arena may also be important sources of *institutional innovation.* The transnational arena is affected by the emergence of new problems, from ecological limits to disease transmission to transnational terrorism. The existing institutional architecture is often inadequate to dealing with those problems, in part because national governments necessarily focus within their own boundaries. Institutional innovations for transnational learning, such as the World Commission on Dams or the Global Compact, or transnational regulation, such as the Kimberly Process or the International Code of Marketing of Breastmilk Substitutes, can emerge from cross-sector struggles that hammer out new arrangements acceptable to and utilizing the resources of diverse stakeholders. As globalization proceeds, the demand for institutional arrangements capable of coping with increased transnational interdependency and ecological scarcities can be expected to increase.

Cross-sector partnerships offer avenues for developing such arrangements. Different sectors bring different strengths to work on transnational problems; cross-sector partnerships offer ways to dovetail those strengths into coalitions that are more than the sum of their parts. CSOs, for example, are good at identifying problems, articulating their value implications, engaging the views of disenfranchised populations, building bridges across differences, and monitoring results.[23] Governments and corporations, in contrast, bring other resources and capacities to transnational problem solving, including greater financial resources, capacities for using them efficiently, legitimate authority and power, and a wide range of other capabilities beyond those of civil society actors.[24] Those capabilities can be vital to identifying and diagnosing problems, articulating desired future states, and constructing institutional arrangements that deal with the emerging global interdependence.

Summary

This chapter has focused on the credibility of cross-sector partnerships that bring together government, business, and civil society actors to solve difficult transnational problems and challenges. These initiatives often have to deal with level and power differences as well as differences in perspective rooted in sector and national backgrounds. But they can be pivotal in solving problems that emerge from increasing global interdependencies and the growing impacts of human activities on the planet.

Assessing the legitimacy and accountabilities of transnational cross-sector initiatives involves negotiations among parties that are diverse in sectoral perspectives as well as in nationality and level. Defining cross-sector missions and strategies requires synthesizing or dovetailing interests to construct partnership missions, managing significant power differences among the partners, and mapping diverse sets of internal and external stakeholders. This assessment process can sometimes recognize previously invisible problem causes and dynamics that affect the legitimacy of partners and of the partnership as a whole. Key bases for legitimacy of cross-sector partnerships include performance and normative concerns, with demonstrated impacts, resources, and constituencies as critical resources for building that legitimacy. Constructing compelling desired futures is necessary to engage partners across sectors, but it may require artful integration of diverse interests and perspectives.

Enhancing the legitimacy of cross-sector partnerships requires spanning a broad range of legitimacy standards and contexts represented by multiple participants, but it may also benefit from the association with so much diversity. Performance legitimacy is key for such partnerships, often defined in quite different terms by diverse stakeholders. To some extent a partnership can build legitimacy by conforming, informing, and associating its work with existing standards held by different sectors. But often, emerging problem areas will require the construction of new standards and expectations for assessing the partnership's work.

Constructing cross-sector accountability systems may be particularly important when the partnership seeks to solve highly charged and controversial problems. An initial challenge is to negotiate expectations with internal and external stakeholders. Those negotiations help define the identity of the partnership and its public visibility. Creating performance measures that make sense across sectors is central to monitoring and assessing performance: important measures include indicators of problem improvement, gains for partners, improved relationships across sectors, and more indirect results such as innovations in problem solving. Using those measures to enable performance consequences involves communicating results to internal and external stakeholders and enabling use of sanctions to hold partners accountable—not a small task given the often large power inequalities encompassed by many partnerships. Finally cross-sector organizational arrangements are necessary if the problem requires ongoing management. Organizational issues include managing the differences among the partners, accomplishing partnership tasks, and revising the organization in response to experience or changing contexts.

Cross-sector accountability systems can be used to enhance partnership legitimacy, to expand operational capacity, and to foster strategic learning to produce more public value on the focal problem. More generally, cross-sector accountability systems can contribute to enhancing public awareness of unrecognized problems, synthesizing widely held aspirations for the future, and catalyzing institutional innovations appropriate to a globalizing world that is increasingly interdependent across sectors, levels, and countries.

Notes

1. Smillie, Ian, "Not Accountable to Anyone? Collective Action and the Role of NGOs in the Campaign to Ban 'Blood Diamonds,'" in *Global Accountabilities: Participation, Pluralism and Public Ethics*, ed. Alnoor Ebrahim and Edwin Weisband (Cambridge, UK: Cambridge University Press, 2007): 112–130.

2. See Partnership Africa Canada, "The Kimberly Controls: How Effective?" Available at http://blooddiamond.pacweb.org/ kimberlyprocess/ (retrieved March 18, 2007).

3. For discussion of the possibilities of altruism and philanthropy-based partnerships between business and civil society organizations, see Austin, J., "Strategic Collaboration between Nonprofits and Businesses," *Nonprofit and Voluntary Sector Quarterly*, 29, no. 1 (2000): 69–97; Austin, J. E., *The Collaboration Challenge: How Nonprofits and Businesses Succeed through Strategic Alliances* (Boston: Harvard Business School, 2000); and Austin, J., Reficco, E., Berger, G., Fischer, R. M., Gutierrez, R., Koljatic, M., Lozano, G. and Ogliastri, E., eds., *Social Partnering in Latin America: Lessons Drawn from Collaborations of Businesses and Civil Society Organizations* (Cambridge, MA: Harvard University Press, 2004). For examples of cross-sector partnerships growing out of initial conflicts, see Brown, L. D. and Ashman, D., "Participation, Social Capital and Intersectoral Problem-Solving: African and Asian Cases," *World Development*, 24, no. 9 (1996): 1467–1479; Brown, L. D. and Ashman, D., "Social Capital, Mutual Influence, and Social Learning in Intersectoral Problem-Solving," in *Organizational Dimensions of Global Change*, ed. D. Cooperrider and J. Dutton (Thousand Oaks, CA: Sage Publications, 1999): 139–167; and Weber, E., *Bringing Society Back In: Grassroots Ecosystem Management, Accountability and Sustainable Communities* (Cambridge, MA: MIT Press, 2003).

4. An example is the international campaign to regulate the marketing of infant formula in developing countries where the lack of safe water supply can result in unnecessary infant deaths from diarrhea. See Johnson, D. A., "Confronting Corporate Power: Strategies and Phases of the Nestle Boycott," in *Research in Corporate Social Performance and Policy*, vol. 8, ed. L. Preston and J. Post, (Greenwich, CT: JAI Press, 1986): 323–344.

5. See, for example, Publish What You Pay and Revenue Watch Institute, *Eye on EITI: Civil Society Perspectives and Recommendations on the Extractive Industries Transparency Initiative* (London and New York: Publish What You Pay and Revenue Watch Institute, 2006).

6. Khagram, S., "An Innovative Experiment in Global Governance: The World Commission on Dams," in *International Commissions and the Power of Ideas*, ed. R. Thakyur, A. Cooper and J. English (Tokyo: UN University Press, 2005): 203–231.

7. Ruggie, John Gerard, "The Theory and Practice of Learning Networks: Corporate Social Responsibility and the Global Compact," *Journal of Corporate Citizenship*, 5 (2002).

8. Reinicke, W. and Deng, F., *Critical Choices: The United Nations, Networks and the Future of Global Governance* (Ottawa: International Development Research Centre, 2000).

9. See Rischard, J. F., *High Noon: Twenty Global Problems, Twenty Years to Solve Them* (New York: Basic Books, 2002).

10. Smillie, "Not Accountable to Anyone?" (2007).

11. Bryson, J. M., Crosby, B. C. and Stone, M. M., "The Design and Implementation of Cross-Sector Collaborations: Propositions from the

Literature," *Public Administration Review*, 66, Supplement (2006): 44–55. See for a prescient analysis of this pattern: Emery, F. and Trist, E., "The Causal Texture of Organizational Environments," *Human Relations*, 18 (1965): 21–32.

12. See Khagram, "An Innovative Experiment in Global Governance" (2005).

13. See Khagram, "An Innovative Experiment in Global Governance" (2005).

14. See materials for developing logical frameworks at WK Kellogg Foundation (http://www.wkkf.org/Pubs/Tools/Evaluation/Pub3669.pdf) and materials on creating change theories at Keystone (http://www.philbandofmercy.org/news_keystone.htm) for examples of approaches to building indicators of change.

15. See Austin, "Strategic Collaboration between Nonprofits and Businesses" (2000) for an analysis of the evolution of social capital and shared values over the course of public-private cooperation. See also Brown and Ashman, "Participation, Social Capital and Intersectoral Problem-Solving" (1996), and "Social Capital, Mutual Influence, and Social Learning in Intersectoral Problem-Solving" (1999) for analysis of the evolution of social capital in government, NGO, and grassroots organization cooperative projects.

16. See Fox, J. A. and Brown, L. D., *The Struggle for Accountability: NGOs, Social Movements and the World Bank* (Cambridge, MA: MIT Press, 1998): Chapter 12.

17. See Rischard, *High Noon*, (2002).

18. Activities by individual partners can create risks to the partnership's reputation and public identity by undermining public trust or relations with external stakeholders. I will use "reputation" and "identity" to reflect the public purposes of these partnerships rather than the private-sector concept of "brand."

19. See for example the work on partnerships and multistakeholder engagement at AccountAbility. http://www.accountability21.net/ (retrieved August 25, 2007).

20. Partnership Africa Canada, "The Kimberly Controls," p. 3.

21. Partnership Africa Canada, "The Kimberly Controls."

22. Johnson, "Confronting Corporate Power" (1986).

23. Brown, L. D. and Timmer, V., "Transnational Civil Society and Social Learning," *Voluntas: International Journal of Voluntary and Nonprofit Organizations*, 17, no. 1 (2006): 1–16.

24. See Brown, L. D., Khagram, S., Moore, M. and Frumkin, P. "Globalization, NGOs, and Multi-Sectoral Relations," in *Governance in a Globalizing World*, ed. J. Nye and J. Donohue (Washington, DC: Brookings Institution, 2000): 271–296; and Rischard, *High Noon*, (2002).

CHAPTER NINE

Civil Society and Transnational Social Learning

This final chapter steps back from the details of organization and domain credibility to explore some of its implications for the transnational arena. The focus is on the consequences of legitimacy and accountability for civil society actors in global governance and problem solving and in the construction of new global institutions and expectations.

This chapter focuses first on the centrality of missions and goals as bases for civil society credibility. Then it briefly describes the processes of establishing legitimacy expectations and accountability standards and their importance in the transnational arena. The third section discusses the consequences of efforts to enhance legitimacy and build accountability systems for civil society organizations (CSOs) and domains. The fourth section focuses on credibility debates as processes for creating and reconstituting concepts and expectations in wider contexts. The final section discusses CSOs as creators of knowledge, meaning, and institutional innovations for dealing with transnational interdependencies, shortages, and emerging governance problems.

The Centrality of Missions and Strategic Goals

In Chapter 1, it was argued that missions and strategic goals are central to articulating the legitimacy and accountabilities of value-based CSOs, given the potentially overwhelming welter of claims and counterclaims that might be mounted by their diverse stakeholders. In the chapters on organization and domain credibility, variations of the strategic triangle were used to organize the assessment of legitimacy and accountability standards, expectations, and aspirations for the future.

The strategic triangle was created to guide leaders of public and nonprofit agencies in making strategic choices. Many CSOs do not think in terms of questions about value creation, legitimacy and support, or organizational capacity, but they do have leaders who make strategic choices on the organization's behalf. For domains, however, decision-making authority for the domain as a whole is often unclear or disputed, so articulating and negotiating shared domain goals may have to precede assessing legitimacy and accountability aspirations or acting collectively to achieve them. For sector associations, the emergence of shared goals is often a response to threats, such as attacks on the legitimacy of international advocacy NGOs or threats to donor support for child sponsorship organizations. Campaign coalitions are often organized to achieve shared goals that unite participants across levels, such as preserving indigenous rights in the campaign against the Mount Apo thermal plant. For cross-sector partnerships, evidence of "sector failure" to solve urgent problems may be a prerequisite for negotiating shared goals, as in the agreements among the government, business and CSO participants in the Kimberly Process to regulate the diamond trade. Building shared domain identity and negotiating shared goals are prerequisites to clarifying domain credibility standards and expectations.

Clarity about goals helps civil society leaders focus their attention on important credibility questions. In transnational contexts, "key stakeholders" may include many actors—private or public funders, regulators from many governments, beneficiaries in many countries, and a wide range of allies or competitors—from many locations and levels. Explicitly managing legitimacy or accountability with all these stakeholders is a Herculean task. It is understandable that many civil society actors have avoided credibility challenges that involve so many stakeholders, since they are already short of resources to carry out difficult missions. When necessary, serious efforts can be launched to deal with legitimacy or accountability issues that are vital to those missions.

But there are at least four reasons for investing resources in credibility issues *before* they become critical. First, these issues are becoming recognized as increasingly serious threats. As credibility issues gain momentum in the transnational arena, reactive stances can become very costly to CSOs and domains. Cleaning up the mess after a debacle may be much more expensive than preventing it if the concern can be predicted ahead of time. Second, focusing attention on legitimacy and accountability can align the expectations of critical stakeholders with strategic goals. Such negotiations can reduce misunderstanding about expectations and mobilize stakeholders to support achieving strategic goals. Third, attention to legitimacy, and particularly to accountability systems, can be the basis for learning that improves value creation and operational capacity as well as legitimacy. These first three reasons for investing proactively in credibility issues have been discussed in some detail in earlier chapters. The fourth reason, discussed in this chapter, is that engaging credibility questions offers opportunities to shape wider debates on the roles of civil society in transnational governance and problem solving. These debates can contribute to framing and constructing an international order that can deal with growing interdependence and emerging global problems.

Constructing Legitimacy Expectations and Domain Standards

Standards for legitimacy and accountability are sometimes set by administrative decisions that define expectations in statutes or in regulations based on expert knowledge. In other circumstances, legitimacy and accountability expectations are constructed in political and social negotiations over arguments in extended discourses that generate new standards and expectations to shape future actions. Those actions may in turn set off future arguments, discourses, and changes in expectations and standards.

Social construction processes for negotiating agreements on legitimacy and accountability among diverse parties are particularly important in the transnational arena, where no superordinate authority exists on most issues and emerging problems are characterized by novelty, large power differences, and contention across boundaries. New concepts and standards, such as the "precautionary principle" for regulating persistent organic pollutants[1] or the "triple bottom line" for measuring corporate performance in social and environmental as well as financial terms,[2] have grown out of multisector arguments and discourses about problems and their solutions. Discourses across sectors and countries can construct new standards and expectations as well as new institutions to enforce them.

Emerging standards can be validated by stakeholder acceptance over time as well as by legal agreements and treaties ratified by national authorities. The process of constructing new standards may be contentious and uneven. Although most countries have signed the Universal Declaration of Human Rights, many continue to dispute its meaning and argue for their own implementation standards.[3] But over time new norms and expectations can emerge from transnational debates and discourses, such as the gradual shift in norms of acceptance of slavery—a target of perhaps the earliest transnational civil society campaign—over the last hundred and fifty years.[4] The social and political construction of new standards and expectations is messier and more ambiguous than the administrative promulgation of new rules—but in arenas that lack superordinate authorities there may be few alternatives.

Changing Legitimacy and Accountability: Is It Worth the Cost?

At the *organization* level, grappling with legitimacy issues or constructing accountability systems can be a costly business. Assessing organizational legitimacy and accountability, enhancing legitimacy, and constructing accountability systems requires resources and demands attention from senior leaders. Being more explicit about legitimacy expectations and accountability standards may make an organization more vulnerable to external criticism, especially if it sets unrealistic performance goals. Accountability systems can impose implementation burdens and create constraints that do not plague competitors. So it is not surprising that CSOs do not rush to grapple with the issues until credibility problems threaten to impose serious costs.

On the other hand, assessing and enhancing organizational legitimacy and accountability can produce valuable results. Assessing legitimacy and accountability requires that the CSO clarify its strategy and value-creation processes and identify its key stakeholders. Enhancing legitimacy involves identifying bases of legitimacy, demonstrating compliance with existing standards, or constructing appropriate new expectations. Creating accountability systems requires developing indicators, negotiating expectations with stakeholders, assessing and monitoring performance, and enabling consequences for that performance. These activities can improve responses to credibility questions, enhance operational capacity, and enable strategic learning about value creation.

Grappling with organizational legitimacy and accountability can also energize debates that change how organizations understand and carry out their missions and strategies. Debates over legitimacy and accountability within Oxfam International have catalyzed significant changes in internal priorities and power relations and have focused attention on coordination across humanitarian and local development projects as well as across policy campaigns. Questions of legitimacy and accountability can fundamentally affect how an organization and its members understand and act on organizational strategies and goals.

At the *domain* level, legitimacy and accountability questions can demand significant time and resources from organizational leaders: they may create new vulnerabilities to external criticism, they may increase brand risk by making the domain more visible and easier to criticize, they may constrain or raise the costs of innovation, they may subject small members to standards that better fit large members, and so on. These drawbacks contribute to the common reluctance among domain leaders to grapple with credibility issues unless they become crises. Action to prevent potential threats can be even more difficult at the domain level than at the organization level.

On the other hand, dealing with credibility challenges can enhance domain capacities. Negotiating agreements on legitimacy and accountability standards helped the sector, campaign, and cross-sector initiatives described in earlier chapters to clarify shared values and interests, to build social capital among domain members, to learn from each other's experience, to make use of each other's diverse resources, and to build capacity for cohesive action against threats to the domain. Creating account-ability systems can help regulate potentially harmful actions by domain members and provide standards by which to claim legitimacy with exter-nal stakeholders.

Debates and negotiations over domain legitimacy and accountability may lead to change in fundamental aspects of the domain. Helping mem-bers recognize their common domain may be a fundamental intervention, particularly for organizations that have seen each other as competitors or opponents. Articulating shared goals and collective strategies can reframe how domain members see their goals and their relationships to other domain members as well as to external stakeholders. Credibility problems can press members to adopt a mutual accountability model that obligates them to account to each other for achieving a larger goal. Even where mutual accountability does not dominate domain relations, as in the Kimberly cross-sector partnership, the experience of negotiating common understanding of the problem and shared strategies for solving it can sig-nificantly change the way the parties understand each other and shape their transnational context in the future.

Legitimacy and Accountability Discourses and the Transnational Context

Debates and negotiations over the legitimacy and accountability of transnational civil society actors can *redefine and reconstitute the standards and expectations of the fields in which they operate.* These debates can produce and legitimate new standards and expectations, which in turn shape actions and the emergence of new arguments and discourses that consol-idate or further change standards and expectations. As we have seen, those negotiations must deal with national differences, diverse levels and sectors, power inequalities, resource scarcities, histories of conflict, poorly understood problems, and a variety of other challenges in order to con-struct widely accepted standards and expectations.

Over time, events at many levels interact to construct transnational standards. Evolving standards for assessing organizational performance, for example, have emerged from debates among different sectors over the years to develop standards for assessing social and environmental impacts as well as financial performance. While these initiatives influ-enced the behavior of individual organizations, they also produced a bewildering variety of standards across organizations and information demands from their stakeholders. The Global Reporting Initiative helped to coalesce this confusion into shared definitions and a reporting process for assessing the "triple bottom line," backed up by a multistakeholder assessment process to ensure its relevance to many stakeholders.[5] While the initial focus of this effort was a multisector campaign to clarify standards and expectations for corporate performance, the discourse has influenced perceptions and expectations in wider contexts. International advocacy NGOs and networks have included elements of the "triple bottom line" in their Accountability Charter and are working with the Global Reporting Initiative to build a reporting system that will be credible across many interested stakeholders.

Figure 9.1 portrays the interaction of actions, ideas and arguments, debates and discourses, and standards and expectations at multiple levels. The concentric circles represent the organizational, domain, and transnational arena levels of analysis. The dotted arrows indicate the links in cycles of actions, arguments, discourses, and standards at different levels.

Figure 9.1 Constructing Legitimacy and Accountability Across Levels

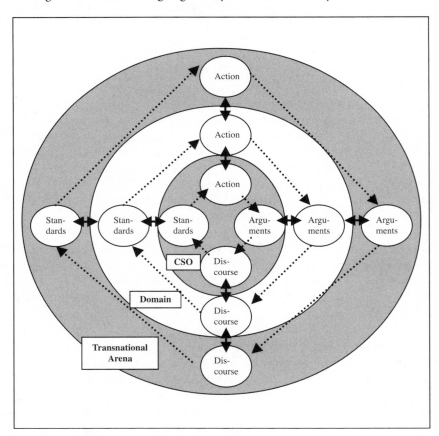

As suggested in Chapter 3, these cycles can produce new legitimacy expectations or "negotiated accountabilities" for organizations and domains. As international advocacy NGOs and networks respond to their own and others' actions with new arguments and ideas about legitimacy and accountability, they modify existing discourses in ways that may construct new standards and expectations.

Events at different levels may influence each other, as indicated by the solid arrows in Figure 9.1. It is common for expectations and standards at macro levels (such as the transnational arena) to shape those at the meso levels (such as domains) or micro levels (such as organizations). Discourses and expectations in transnational contexts and domains influence particular CSOs, as indicated by their concern with credibility challenges. But it is also possible for influence to flow from micro to macro levels, as organizational actions and arguments affect the emergence of new domain or transnational arguments, discourses and standards.

Transparency International, for example, has reshaped international discourses and standards on corruption, and the Global Reporting Initiative is constructing new standards and processes for assessing organizational performance. These new standards have reverberations both at the domain level, such as the reporting practices of extractive industries, and in the transnational context, such as changes in international treaties about the acceptability of corrupt business initiatives. One implication of Figure 9.1 is that discourses and institutions at the transnational level can affect civil society actors at the national and local levels. Another is that strategically positioned civil society actors can influence transnational standards and expectations that will shape the future actions of many other actors. The solid arrows linking the cycles at different levels reflect this potential for two-way influence across levels.

Debates within and across levels can alter legitimacy and accountability standards for CSOs and many other actors. Where standards and expectations are underdeveloped or emerging, organizational arguments and ideas can contribute to changing domain standards, and domain debates and controversies may change expectations in wider contexts.

Transnational debates and discourses about legitimacy and accountability may also *reshape governance processes* within and across levels. Within organizations, decisions about legitimacy challenges and accountability claims may be made by organizational authorities. But those authorities have limited capacities to impose their preferences on external stakeholders or wider domains. Legitimacy expectations are elements of a "negotiated order" beyond the organization that turns on debates and discourses among stakeholders who can be influenced, but not controlled, by organizational leaders. In domains and wider contexts, legitimacy standards and expectations emerge from actions, arguments, and discourses among many independent actors, who are driven by their own concerns and interests. These debates can generate better understanding of processes for constructing standards in the transnational context—which stakeholders must be consulted, how conflicts and disagreements can be managed, what social and organizational capital is essential, and what steps are most likely to produce useful and accepted results. The development of a systematic multistakeholder process for defining reporting standards, for example, has been hailed as a major contribution of the Global Reporting Initiative. That process allows adaptation and development of reporting criteria as circumstances change, without the criteria losing their widespread legitimacy.

A third important contribution of these transnational debates can be the *reconstruction of concepts of legitimacy and accountability*. The struggles over the legitimacy and accountability of CSOs have drawn attention to the wide range of stakeholders with accountability claims, in contrast to the clearer definition of the primary accountabilities for the government and business sectors. One solution to this issue is to redefine and simplify civil society responsibilities to define their primary accountabilities. But another alternative is for business organizations and government agencies to recognize the multiplicity of stakeholders with possible accountability claims on them.[6] Perhaps corporations should be more accountable to stakeholders beyond their owners, and governments should attend to the claims of constituents other than voting citizens. The debates on civil society legitimacy and accountability may produce more complex and differentiated conceptions of organizational obligations to contexts and stakeholders that illuminate the credibility challenges facing other sectors as well.

Reframing accountability and legitimacy concepts can also reconstitute the experience of those who employ them. It has been argued that the emphasis on agency theory in the corporate sector has created the very problems it seeks to manage, as agents have focused on maximizing their own interests within the contracts designed to constrain those interests.[7] The skyrocketing compensation to corporate chief executives, independent of their contributions to the viability of their organizations, reflects a perversion of the intentions underlying their contracts.[8] The effort to control agent opportunism may have reinforced the tendency for agents to develop sophisticated ways to subvert those controls. If accountability standards both regulate and encourage certain forms of behavior, it might benefit domains and the transnational context to emphasize, where possible, wider use of mutual accountability models that focus attention on developing shared analyses and goals and building trust and mutual influence as critical elements of interorganizational and interpersonal relations. The choice of accountability concepts over time will shape the experience of participants, their understanding of "appropriate behavior," and the cognitive legitimacy of different standards.

Legitimacy and Accountability in an Evolving Transnational Society

The issues of legitimacy and accountability in the transnational arena have emerged as major concerns for many actors beyond civil society— transnational corporations and intergovernmental institutions also struggle to establish and preserve their legitimacy and grapple with their accountabilities to various stakeholders. The standards, norms, values, and expectations that emerge from these debates and discourses potentially shape behavior in the transnational arena for many sectors. Intersectoral debates and decisions about use of the precautionary principle to regulate persistent organic pollutants, the standards for constructing large dams, and the assessment of the triple bottom line all illustrate the construction of standards to guide transnational actors even in the absence of a global authority to establish and enforce decisions.[9] We are seeing the evolution of transnational institutions in response to emerging challenges that cannot be managed by existing arrangements.

The creation of credibility standards and expectations for transnational civil society actors is an aspect of this larger process. Their accountability and legitimacy is pivotal to positioning CSOs to raise issues and to challenge other actors in an increasingly globalized world. Enhancing legitimacy and constructing accountability systems are essential to maintaining the public trust that enables civil society actors to catalyze public debate about transnational issues.[10]

At the heart of civil society influence on transnational issues is the capacity of CSOs to inform larger publics of critical issues and help construct the meaning of those issues.[11] The creation of meaning involves identifying issues, framing their value implications, demonstrating their consequences, mobilizing concerned publics, articulating options, and campaigning for actions to preserve and implement widely held values.[12] Civil society actors can provide information, construct arguments, enable testimony by key actors, and interpret complex events in terms that are comprehensible and compelling to wider publics. CSOs are often active and influential participants in transnational campaigns that mobilize participants across national and sector boundaries to press for goals such as disarmament treaties, land mine bans, human rights protection, World Bank reforms, and expansion of women's rights.[13] So transnational CSOs can play important roles in raising, interpreting, and acting on global concerns.

More importantly, this analysis suggests that transnational civil society actors are contributing to defining legitimacy and accountability regimes that affect a wide range of transnational institutions. Debates over construction of large dams, corporate marketing practices, sustainability performance, preservation of human rights, and control of genocide have all reshaped standards and expectations, albeit with varying degrees of success. These debates, in part because of civil society intervention, have sometimes reshaped power asymmetries that muted grassroots voices and have created new access to decision makers.

By recognizing the importance of legitimacy and accountability, civil society actors may be altering credibility discourses for business and government institutions as well as for themselves. International advocacy NGOs and networks, skeptical about corporate self-regulation as a vehicle for ensuring compliance, are working to create more credible methods of monitoring and sanctioning civil society abuses—and so are reinforcing expectations for corporate and government legitimacy and accountability as well. Efforts to construct greater credibility for transnational CSOs can shape the domains in which they are embedded—and so can build mechanisms and set expectations for wider transnational legitimacy and accountability regimes for many actors.

Notes

1. Maguire, S. and Hardy, C., "The Emergence of New Global Institutions: A Discursive Perspective," *Organization Studies*, 27, no. 1 (2006): 7–29.

2. Brown, H. S., de Jong, M. and Lessidrenska, T., "The Rise of the Global Reporting Initiative (GRI) as a Case of Institutional Entrepreneurship," Working Paper No. 36, Corporate Social Responsibility Initiative, John F. Kennedy School of Government, Harvard University, May 2007.

3. Risse, Thomas, "The Power of Norms versus the Norms of Power: Transnational Civil Society and Human Rights," in *The Third Force*, ed. Ann Florini (Washington, DC: Carnegie Endowment, 2001): 177–210.

4. Keck, Margaret and Sikkink, Kathryn, *Activists Beyond Borders* (Ithaca, NY: Cornell University Press, 1998).

5. Brown, de Jong and Lessidrenska, "The Rise of the Global Reporting Initiative (GRI) as a Case of Institutional Entrepreneurship" (2007).

6. For stakeholder theories of business organizations, see Freeman, R. E., *Strategic Management: A Stakeholder Approach* (Boston: Pitman, 1984); Post, J. E., Preston, L. E. and Sachs, S., *Redefining the Corporation: Stakeholder Management and Organizational Wealth* (Stanford, CA: University of Stanford Press, 2002). For exploration of the range of accountabilities that might be relevant to government agencies, see

Behn, Robert D., *Rethinking Democratic Accountability* (Washington, DC: Brookings Institution Press, 2001); Moore, Mark H., *Creating Public Value: Strategic Management in Government* (Cambridge, MA: Harvard University Press, 1995).

7. See Roberts, John, "Trust and Control in Anglo-American Systems of Corporate Governance: The Individualizing and Socializing Effects of Processes of Accountability," *Human Relations*, 54, no. 12 (2001): 1547–1572.

8. Yankelovich, D., *Profit with Honor: The New Stage of Market Capitalism* (New Haven, CT: Yale University Press, 2006).

9. On the emergence of the "precautionary principle," see Maguire and Hardy, "The Emergence of New Global Institutions" (2006). For a description of the World Commission on Dams, see Khagram, S., "An Innovative Experiment in Global Governance: The World Commission on Dams," in *International Commissions and the Power of Ideas*, ed. R. Thakyur, A. Cooper and J. English (Tokyo: UN University Press, 2005): 203–231. For a discussion of the GRI, see Brown, de Jong and Lessidrenska, "The Rise of the Global Reporting Initiative (GRI) as a Case of Institutional Entrepreneurship" (2007).

10. While the annual global surveys by Globescan indicate that civil society actors continue to be more widely trusted that international government organizations, governments, or transnational corporations, the level of public trust of all these institutions has declined over the last five years. See Globescan (2006) "Trust in Institutions" at http://www. globescan.com/rf_ir_trust.htm (retrieved January 5, 2007). Declines may be particularly problematic for civil society actors who depend on their reputations for integrity and commitment to the public interest for their influence with the public and the other sectors.

11. Khagram, Sanjeev, Riker, James V. and Sikkink, Kathryn, eds., *Restructuring World Politics: Transnational Social Movements, Networks, and Norms* (Minneapolis: University of Minnesota, 2002).

12. See Brown, L. D. and Timmer, V., "Transnational Civil Society and Social Learning," *Voluntas: International Journal of Voluntary and Nonprofit Organizations*, 17, no. 1 (2006): 1–16.; and Keck and Sikkink, *Activists Beyond Borders* (1998).

13. Batliwala, S. and Brown, L. D., eds., *Transnational Civil Society: An Introduction* (Bloomfield, CT: Kumarian Press, 2006); Fox, J. and Brown, L. D., *The Struggle for Accountability: NGOs, Social Movements, and the World Bank* (Cambridge, MA: MIT Press, 1998).

Glossary

CONAIE	Confederation of Indigenous Nationalities of Ecuador
CSO	Civil Society Organization
EITI	Extractive Industries Transparency Initiative
GRI	Global Reporting Initiative
HAP-I	Humanitarian Accountability Project International
IANGO	International Advocacy NGO or Network
IMF	International Monetary Foundation
KPCS	Kimberly Process Certification Scheme
OECD	Organization for Economic Cooperation and Development
NGO	Non-governmental Organization
North	Refers to "global North" of wealthy industrialized countries
PCNC	Philippines Council for NGO Certification
South	Refers to "global South" of poor and developing countries
TI	Transparency International
WTO	World Trade Organization

About the Author

L. David Brown is Associate Director for International Programs at the Hauser Center for Nonprofit Organizations and Lecturer in Public Policy at the Kennedy School of Government. Prior to coming to Harvard he was President and Co-Founder (with Jane Covey) of the Institute for Development Research, a nonprofit center for development research and consultation, and Professor of Organizational Behavior at Boston University. His research and consulting have focused on institutional development, particularly for civil society organizations and networks, that fosters sustainable development and social transformation. He has been a Fulbright Lecturer in India and a Peace Corps community organizer in Ethiopia and is currently learning to be a doting grandparent.

Index

Also from Kumarian Press . . .

Civil Society and NGOs:

Transnational Civil Society: An Introduction
Edited by Srilatha Batliwala and L. David Brown

CIVICUS Global Survey of the State of Civil Society, Vol. 2
Edited by V. Finn Heinrich and Lorenzo Fioramonti

Creating a Better World: Interpreting Global Civil Society
Edited by Rupert Taylor

Humanitarian Alert: NGO Information and Its Impact on US Foreign Policy
Abby Stoddard

New and Forthcoming:

The World Bank and the Gods of Lending
Steve Berkman

Surrogates of the State: NGOs, Development and Ujamaa in Tanzania
By Michael Jennings

World Disasters Report 2007: Focus on Discrimination
Edited by Yvonne Klynman, Nicholas Kouppari and Mohammed Mukhier

Peace through Health: How Health Professionals Can Work for a Less Violent World
Edited by Neil Arya and Joanna Santa Barbara

Visit Kumarian Press at **www.kpbooks.com** or call **toll-free 800.232.0223** for a complete catalog

green press
INITIATIVE

Kumarian Press is committed to preserving ancient forests and natural resources. We elected to print this title on 30% post consumer recycled paper, processed chlorine free. As a result, for this printing, we have saved:

4   Trees (40' tall and 6-8" diameter)
1,293   Gallons of Wastewater
2 million   BTU's of Total Energy
166   Pounds of Solid Waste
311   Pounds of Greenhouse Gases

Kumarian Press made this paper choice because our printer, Thomson-Shore, Inc., is a member of Green Press Initiative, a nonprofit program dedicated to supporting authors, publishers, and suppliers in their efforts to reduce their use of fiber obtained from endangered forests.

For more information, visit www.greenpressinitiative.org

Environmental impact estimates were made using the Environmental Defense Paper Calculator. For more information visit: www.papercalculator.org.

 Kumarian Press, located in Sterling, Virginia, is a forward-looking, scholarly press that promotes active international engagement and an awareness of global connectedness.